Different But Equal: Documenting the Contribution of Dissident Scholars

Edited by
Daniel Sutter

WILEY-BLACKWELL

Different But Equal: Documenting the Contribution of Dissident Scholars

Edited by

Daniel Sutter

WILEY-BLACKWELL

This edition first published 2012

Registered Office
John Wiley & Sons Ltd, The Atrium, Southern Gate, Chichester, West Sussex, PO19 8SQ, United Kingdom

Editorial Offices
350 Main Street, Malden, MA 02148-5020, USA
9600 Garsington Road, Oxford, OX4 2DQ, UK
The Atrium, Southern Gate, Chichester, West Sussex, PO19 8SQ, UK

For details of our global editorial offices, for customer services, and for information about how to apply for permission to reuse the copyright material in this book, please see our website at www.wiley.com/wiley-blackwell.

Library of Congress Cataloging-in-Publication Data

Different but equal : documenting the contribution of dissident scholars / edited by Daniel Sutter.
p. cm.
Originally published as: "The American journal of economics and sociology, November 2012 Issue.
Includes index.
ISBN 978-1-118-54275-0—ISBN 978-1-118-54278-1 1. Economics. 2. Economic policy. I. Sutter, Daniel. II. American journal of economics and sociology.
HB171.D633 2012
330—dc23

2012040555

A catalogue record for this book is available from the Library of Congress.

Set in 10 on 13pt Garamond Light by Toppan Best-set Premedia Limited
Printed in Singapore by Markono Print Media Pte Ltd.

01—2012

Contents

Different but Equal? On the Contribution of Dissident Economists

By DANIEL SUTTER*

ABSTRACT. The availability of publication and citation databases facilitate construction of rankings of economics journals, economists, and departments. Mainstream economists typically find the research questions and methods of heterodox economists dubious, and this reaction creates a bias against heterodox research in peer review, which extends to traditional bibliometric rankings. University administrators interested in improving the quality of the economics department, as conventionally measured, will see heterodox economists as a liability. But establishing the bias of conventional metrics of scholarship quality and the consequences of these biases does not establish the comparable worth of the contributions of dissident economists. This special issue seeks innovated ways to document the relative quality of the contributions of dissident economists.

Introduction

Science is conducted within a paradigm, a shared set of assumptions or framework (Kuhn 1996). A paradigm designates open research questions while setting others aside; any research framework must take some facts as given, and the givens determine the relevant types of evidence. Normal science occurs within a discipline's dominant paradigm. A dominant paradigm is never the only way to organize research, but scholars rejecting the dominant paradigm risk marginalization. The dominance of a paradigm at a point in time does not ensure its permanence, as the accumulation of contradictory evidence eventually can spark a paradigm shift.

The wisdom of crowds suggests that the consensus of experts in a discipline—meaning the mainstream paradigm—represents the best method of pursuing knowledge. Yet a crowd of academics may not be

*Manuel H. Johnson Center for Political Economy, Troy University, Troy, AL 36082, Tel: (334) 670-5771, E-mail: dsutter@troy.edu.

American Journal of Economics and Sociology, Vol. 71, No. 5 (November, 2012).

as wise as the typical crowd. Only those trained in a discipline get to weigh-in on the relative value of mainstream and dissident paradigms. The graduate training selection process violates the independence of evaluation required for information aggregation (Sutter 2007). And even if the mainstream has the highest probability of yielding understanding of any school of thought, this probability is well less than one.

In the academy, the overlap of departmental and disciplinary boundaries reinforces the insulating effect of a paradigm, as disciplines attempt to protect their turf against others (Davis 2008). Scholars whose research does not fit within a discipline's dominant paradigm will face an added challenge succeeding in this field within the academy. And many disciplines essentially exclude scholars without university faculty appointments. The organization of disciplines within the academy is more likely to produce groupthink than truly independent judgments (Klein and Stern 2009).

Although many commentators decry liberal domination of the Ivory Tower, the dominant paradigm in most disciplines is typically methodological. In economics the dominant methodology combines formal (mathematical) modeling and econometric testing. The method marginalizes social forces not amenable to mathematical analysis, like entrepreneurship, institutions, transactions costs, social capital, and class relations. The dominant methodology also reduces other forms of inquiry to insignificance, such as qualitative research, historical research, and case studies. As a consequence, scholars working in Austrian, property rights, transactions costs, Marxist, and other heterodox traditions face methodological discrimination in publishing in mainstream journals and often have to publish in specialized journals. A dominant paradigm is even more of a threat in a contested discipline like economics (Elsner and Lee 2010). The methodological elements of the dominant paradigm in a contested discipline create the danger that the paradigm serves to prevent research critical of the prevailing economic system for ideological reasons.

The best method for economists to conduct their inquiries is a topic seemingly of interest and relevance only for academics. But academic scribblers affect events outside the academy, particularly in a policy relevant discipline like economics. The economics profession provides guidance for economic policy. The profession's failing can have serious consequences for society. The potential shortcomings of economics have consequences well beyond the walls of the Ivory Tower. Economics' failure to provide timely explanations for the Great Depression and the financial crisis of 2008 illustrate the cost to society of the economics profession being too locked into the mainstream paradigm. Events in the world will sometimes defy explanation within the dominant paradigm. While such events can set a paradigm shift in motion, in a policy relevant discipline they leave society without guidance. Often heterodox or dissident schools of thought can provide insight for events incomprehensible to the mainstream. Dissident thinkers will have greater impact on contemporary society if their works inspire active schools of thought instead of collecting dust on library shelves.

Dissident schools of thought in economics (or other disciplines) consequently provide great value to the field and at certain times to society. And yet heterodox economists and schools of thought face greater pressure within the academy today than in recent years. The reason is a relatively benign desire to document quality of research output. Metrics exist to measure the quality of scholarship, but they are biased against heterodox economists. Conventional metrics based either on peer evaluation of prestige or citation analysis, will rate heterodox journals as inferior to mainstream journals. The bias against research outside of the mainstream tradition in peer review extends thus to the metrics of research quality.

This special issue considers how to document the contribution of dissident economists. In this introduction I review how conventional metrics of research quality fail to accurately measure the contribution of dissidents relative to the mainstream. The biased metrics of scholarship combine with a collective goods problem to create a hostile environment for heterodox economists at research universities. I then discuss some recent attempts to document the contribution of dissident economists before previewing the papers in this issue.

University Support for Faculty Research

Knowledge is a public good, and universities provide the major financial support for the generation of knowledge in many disciplines.

The support takes the form of reduced teaching loads, library resources, funding for travel, and respect for the research product. Tuition payers, donors, and for public universities taxpayers, ultimately fund faculty research. The cross-subsidization of research is rationalized in part by spillovers between faculty research and teaching, but the societal (if not necessarily market) value of research provides the more compelling rationale, together with the low cost of joint production at a university. The rising cost of higher education (Vedder 2004) has understandably led to increased demands for evidence of effectiveness from universities. For administrators to require evidence of research output or allocate resources to faculty or departments producing more and better research is applaudable.

Consider the situation of a university administrator responsible for economics, among other disciplines. The development of metrics of research quality provide administrators with no expertise in a discipline a means to verify claims of faculty about the quality or impact of their research. And yet measures of research quality have changed economics and other disciplines. Cantor (2009) describes English departments in the U.S. in the 1950s as exhibiting considerable within-department homogeneity and yet the discipline as a whole was quite diverse, with many distinct schools of thought. The creation of national and global markets for research faculty has increased the homogeneity of research departments. Rankings of journals, economists, and departments, greatly facilitated by electronic databases, play a large role in this process. Without the Social Science Citation Index, Econ Lit, and other publication databases, dissident economists could point to their scholarly articles and books to keep administrators happy.

Once departments can readily be ranked, administrators will consult the rankings. In the U.K. this has been formalized through the Research Assessment Exercise (RAE), used then to allocate resources among universities (Lee 2007). U.S. higher education is more decentralized, but measures of productivity like the National Research Council's (NRC) doctoral program rankings are highly influential among administrators (Holcombe 2004). NRC rankings and journal impact factors represent a consistent methodology applied across a wide range of disciplines, and can become focal for administrators from different disciplines. Government grants, used in ranking research universities, strengthen a mainstream bias, as heterodox economists are unlikely to receive support from mainstream dominated funding sources like the National Science Foundation. All of these factors have combined to create an environment hostile to heterodox economists at research universities. Administrators seeking to build a highly ranked department, conventionally measured, might move to replace productive heterodox economists, despite no animus toward heterodox economics.

The basis of the bias of conventional measures of research quality against dissident scholars deserves elaboration. Peer review allows for evaluation of knowledge claims by specialists; if evaluation of arguments offered by economists (or sociologists, or epidemiologists) requires specialized training, only peers with this training and expertise can evaluate research. Peer review is the distinguishing quality of scholarly research. Documenting scholarly research output is a relatively easy task for administrators—simply verify the peer-review process of the journal or publisher. The challenge arises in documenting the quality of research, or identifying the most important research contributions, and over a relatively short time frame. Important contributions can be easily identified in retrospect, but this provides no guidance for hiring or tenure decisions today.

The quality of a scholar's contributions can be measured using journal rankings, citations, or peer evaluation of the overall research record. Such metrics of scholarship struggle to properly measure the contribution of dissident scholars. Journal rankings, citations, and reputation derive from judgments of the quality of research. Economists will apply their own standards of what constitutes good research, and most often these will be the standards of their school of thought. Thus mainstream economists will use mainstream standards, and likely to judge heterodox research as low quality relative to these standards. While mainstream economists might accurately identify high- or low-quality mainstream research, they will evaluate heterodox economics as low quality simply because the research does not apply methods or address questions the mainstream paradigm considers appropriate. Heterodox economists will also apply personal values in peer review and likely dismiss mainstream research as of low quality. The mainstream scholar's judgment of dissident research as low quality relative to mainstream standards really provides no new information.

Conventional metrics of the quality of scholarly output essentially aggregate judgments relative to one's own methods. Quality can be measured by querying leading researchers, as the U.K. RAE economics panel did in implicitly utilizing Diamond's (1989) list of top journals. The reputation of economists, largely dependent on having a position at a "leading" university, will depend on being part of the mainstream. Leading mainstream economists tend to discount the contributions of and are more numerous than heterodox economists. Furthermore, given their substantial differences (Holcombe 2008), heterodox economists will not speak with one voice. Conventional metrics essentially repackage the information that a given economist or journal is heterodox in evaluations across schools of thought. They provide no independent evidence of superior quality of mainstream scholarship.

This argument also applies to citations. In principle citations indicate the research a scholar draws on in writing a paper. Important research will be used more in research, and so citation counts (which exclude self-citations) should measure the importance of research (Laband and Tollison 2000). Yet authors cite research for several reasons: for use in the current research, as a source of authority, to criticize alleged mistakes or faulty inferences, and to distinguish the current research from the existing literature. That critical citations enter positively in a citation count is one weakness of citations (Klein with Chiang 2004). Perhaps more significant in rendering the exercise self-referential, citation to distinguish the current research from prior work is guided by social rules. What counts as relevant literature that must be cited? With over 800 economics journals now in existence, there will be dozens—if not hundreds—of papers on any topic. And most topics have been investigated by other social scientists. What literature must be acknowledged and referenced? Social rules enforced by referees and editors with authority to insist on citation (or delete a reference) answer these questions. Referees will generally apply their personal values in making this determination—meaning that we will view the literature in our school of thought as relevant. Mainstream referees and editors will only require citation of mainstream papers.

And citation of too many papers in the *Review of Austrian Economics* or the *Review of Radical Political Economy* will convince editors and referees that the paper is not appropriate for a mainstream journal. Leading mainstream journals will not cite heterodox journals even for papers directly on topic. Mainstream journals end up importing few citations from but do export citations to heterodox journals, and will be judged superior in a citation analysis. Yet the analysis simply documents conventions in citation. Metrics of quality are largely self-referential and provide little if any actual evidence of the superiority of mainstream research.[1]

The pressures for homogeneity have consequences for the economics profession. The profession as a whole is healthier when active dissident schools of thought complement the mainstream. Heterodox approaches challenge the assumptions of and occasionally inject ideas into the mainstream. Dissident schools of thought can offer guidance when world events defy explanation by the mainstream. And dissidents can facilitate scientific revolutions by providing a coherent, viable alternative paradigm. Heterodox schools of thought are more likely to make these contributions if there is a critical mass of academic economists actively researching in these traditions. Maintaining an active presence in the academic or professional economics community requires maintaining heterodox doctoral programs where future generations of economists can learn how to do research in institutional economics or Marxist economics or Austrian economics.[2]

Heterodox graduate programs have been placed on the endangered species list due largely to pressures generated by conventional metrics of quality. And the process could be driven by administrators with no hostility toward (or knowledge of) heterodox economics. Trying to direct research resources toward the economists most likely to put them to good use could impoverish research in the economics profession. To prevent this, dissident economists must expose the bias (which has largely been accomplished), demonstrate the deleterious effects of homogenization, and document the contribution of dissident economists. Dissident schools of thought essentially provide a public good, contributing to the health of the profession and on occasion benefitting the larger society. But it is costly for a university to house a dissident graduate program, with the costs including a lower rank on conventional metrics, fewer prestigious research grants, and in countries following the U.K.'s RAE lead, fewer resources.

Directions for Documenting Dissident Contributions

Demonstrating the bias of conventional metrics against heterodox economists does not establish the quality of heterodox research. While heterodox economists may think that our research is of equal or greater value as that of the mainstream, university administrators will demand evidence for such obviously self-serving claims. How can the contribution of dissident economists be documented in the face of the bias as infecting conventional measures of research output? This question motivates this special issue of the *American Journal of Economics and Sociology*. Dissidents need to think carefully about how to demonstrate, quantify, or otherwise document the quality of their research.

Two alternatives could be pursued in this endeavor. A first approach could rank heterodox or dissident economists and departments. Heterodox rankings might be sufficient for administrators willing to accept a dissident economist or department, but wanting documentation of the quality of their dissidents relative to other heterodox economists. A second approach would demonstrate the quality of heterodox research relative to the mainstream. This could be done by correcting conventional bibliometric metrics for their mainstream bias or assembling different types of evidence of quality, perhaps qualitative as opposed to the quantitative conventional metrics.

Documenting or measuring the contribution of dissident scholars is a topic of ongoing research, with recent contributions in each of these three directions. Lee (2008) ranks 17 heterodox journals to identify the most productive heterodox economics departments. The journals span several different heterodox traditions (Institutional, Post Keynesian, Radical Political Economy) and he evaluates these journals to devise relative impact factors. Lee's ranking procedure differs from standard metrics in offering normative criteria and evaluating the heterodox journals' performance relative to these values.

An innovative and important recent article by Lee, Grijalva, and Nowell (2010) attempts to de-bias conventional rankings. They add

Lee's (2008) heterodox journal rankings to Grijalva and Nowell's (2007) ranking of U.S. Ph.D. programs by field based on journal article publications. Relative rankings of mainstream and heterodox journals provide a basis for overall rankings, once a comparison point between the two sets of journals is established. They make calculations based on different weights for the top heterodox journals relative to the top mainstream journals. The proper weights cannot be identified in this manner, however, leaving the relative value of heterodox scholarship up in the air.

The value of heterodox economics can also be explored through market demand for heterodox economists. Sutter (2012) examines placements of graduates of out-of-the-mainstream U.S. economics doctoral programs by other U.S. doctoral programs. Not surprisingly Harvard, MIT, Chicago, and other elite universities dominate these prestigious job placements. But heterodox programs perform better than predicted when compared with programs of similar rank and age. In regression analysis heterodox programs have 40 percent to 90 percent more placements than expected, indicating that the job market places value on dissident economists.

An approach not used to date would examine the use of economic research by constituencies outside of academic economics. Outside users will not share the bias of mainstream economists. Absent preconceived notions of what constitutes good economics or pressure to adhere to the discipline's conventions, outside users will seek research meeting their needs. A number of different explorations along these lines are possible. For instance, citations in other academic disciplines to economics journals could be analyzed. The playing field between orthodoxy and heterodoxy should be more evenly balanced but not necessarily level in such a competition. An appropriate test might be if heterodox economists are cited more frequently relative to mainstream economists in, say, sociology or management journals. Another potential external user group could be public policy think tanks, which use research by economists to make policy arguments to a general audience. A citation analysis again could examine the relative use by policy analysts of heterodox and mainstream economics. The news media and opinion columnists could provide another external user group. Even employment of economists as consultants or expert witnesses could conceivably signal the value of the research of heterodox economists.

Overview of the Special Issue

Gene Callahan and Peter Leeson lead off the special issue with a heart-warming tale for dissidents about an approach to scientific inquiry known as mechanical philosophy, which held sway for almost a century in Europe. The mainstream during this time dismissed Newton's theory of gravity as "manifest stupidity," so mainstream scientists scoffed at one of the greatest scientists of all time. Several of the descriptions of mechanical philosophy Callahan and Leeson offer could apply almost with revision to describe mainstream economics today. Examples from the history of science (or social science) can do more than just fuel the dissident scholar; they can hopefully steel the university administrator to retain productive dissident economists and resist the lure of moving up a couple of places in the mainstream rankings.

Richard Wagner examines the production of economic theories, and provides insight into the sources of bias among schools of thought. Economic theory is not produced intentionally by a single person or firm, but rather emerges spontaneously from the interaction of scholars. The organization of the production process thus significantly affects the resulting scholarship. Economics by self-financing amateurs will address the curiosity of the researchers, while external funding injects other considerations into the production process. Wagner notes the typically subtle nature of external effects: government officials will value theories that help them govern, and the lure of being at the seat of power is enough to induce some economists to make their theorizing policy relevant. The academy has successfully avoided direct governmental control over theorizing, with intellectual freedom preserving this control for faculty. Wagner's examination suggests the value of comparative analyses of how the industrial organization of higher education affects biases in academic research. The balance between public and private universities and level of government support universities differ across nations. And the policy relevance of a discipline affects the extent to which external forces seek to influence scholarship. The policy relevance of economics ensures that it will remain a contested discipline, but less policy relevant disciplines should have a different set of biases.

Daniel Klein examines whether economists reach a conclusion in their public statements (including published research) on different policy questions. He specifically conducts a meta-analysis of policy review papers from *Econ Journal Watch*. Klein considers these papers from the contrasting perspectives of the status quo and the liberty (meaning freedom of contract) position. The studies typically review issues where the status quo policy currently restricts individual freedom and markets (for example, rent control and drug prohibition). Klein then labels economists supporting the liberty position (reduced FDA control over pharmaceuticals or medical devices) as dissidents. In nine of his eleven cases, a preponderance of on-the-record statements by economists support the dissident position, so dissidents (again as defined by Klein) dominate the professional discourse. The economics profession at-large, as revealed through surveys, shares the dissident position on several issues, including sports subsidies, drug policy, and human organ liberalization. The strongest evidence of a contribution by dissident economists would be an issue where dissidents eventually won over the mainstream. The reviews and the survey evidence Klein examines are both contemporary, and so clear cases of dissidents winning over the mainstream remains elusive. An interesting extension would examine the evolution of these policy debates over time.

Edward Stringham proposes measuring a scholar's contributions through demand, specifically downloads of papers from the Social Science Research Network (SSRN). McCloskey (1995) argues that papers published in leading journals that are never read are of low quality, despite passing peer review at a prestigious journal. SSRN is a more democratic gatekeeping process than peer review, as any scholar can register and upload working or published papers. The audience can then choose which papers to download (and presumably read) without the intermediation of editors or referees. Given the biases of the publication process, downloads could be a better measure of the value of heterodox economics. The SSRN database has some limitations as a measure of demand: it is an elective repository of papers and many economists do not use SSRN, and is not the only portal through which papers may be available, so SSRN downloads are not full measures of demand. Stringham importantly finds that the free market and Austrian economists he focuses on rank higher on downloads than citations. Citations, as discussed, can be infected with bias, so downloads should be less biased. Downloads of papers from journal websites offer a promising way to measure both the impact of various papers in a particular journal and across different journals. Will heterodox economists and journals do better in rankings based on readership than on conventional bibliometric measures?

The articles by Brian Douglass and Peter Boettke, Alexander Fink, and Daniel Smith examine Nobel prize winners for evidence on trends in scholarship. The two articles use different partitions of prize winners: Douglass uses Meir Kohn's (2004, 2007) division of economics into a value paradigm and exchange paradigm, while Boettke, Fink, and Smith employ Boettke's (2007) characterization of mainline vs. mainstream economists. Both the exchange paradigm and mainline economics trace back to Adam Smith's project of studying economic institutions. The alternatives of the value paradigm or mainline economics seek to rigorously characterize the economy in equilibrium, reducing markets and firms to parametrically given prices and production sets. The exchange paradigm and mainline economics, despite intellectual origins to Smith, definitely became the dissident view by the middle of the 20th century.[3] Douglass examines the awarding of prizes and publications by winners in top economics journals to provide evidence for Kohn's claim that the exchange paradigm has largely supplanted the value paradigm. Boettke, Fink, and Smith focus on Social Science Citation Index (SSCI) citations to the mainline and mainstream prize winners' scholarship. Interestingly, they examine citations from both the annual hard copies and on-line editions of the SSCI and find that the choice of database to measure scholarship affects the contribution even of Nobel laureates. Boettke, Fink, and Smith argue that the mainline laureates have made a more lasting impact on scholarship. Both papers establish that the dissidents won out over the mainstream position of the 1960s and 1970s, demonstrating by example the value of dissident scholarship.

Notes

1. As Kapeller (2010) discusses, the citations that factor into the journal citation reports and impact factors can be manipulated in a number of other ways.

2. Whether clusters of heterodox economists at a doctoral granting program are necessary to turn out a next generation of heterodox economists is ultimately an empirical proposition. The works of Marx or Mises or Veblen are not lost even if not taught currently in graduate economics classes; future economists could always become heterodox economists without formal training. Or perhaps a single heterodox economist at a 40-person doctoral granting department may be sufficient to keep a school alive. I believe that clusters of heterodox scholars, or heterodox doctoral programs, are necessary, but assert this without evidence.

3. Of course, many heterodox economists would probably claim that no economist prominent enough to win a Nobel prize was really a dissident.

References

Boettke, P. B. (2007). "Liberty vs. Power in Economic Policy in the 20th and 21st Centuries." *Journal of Private Enterprise* 22(2): 7–36.

Cantor, P. A. (2009). "When Is Diversity Not Diversity: A Brief History of the English Department." In *The Politically Correct University: Problems, Scope and Reforms.* Eds. R. Maranto, R. E. Redding, and F. M. Hess. Washington, DC: American Enterprise Institute.

Davis, J. B. (2008). "The Turn in Economics and Return of Orthodoxy." *Cambridge Journal of Economics* 32(3): 349–366.

Diamond, A. M. (1989). "The Core Journals of Economics" *Current Contents* 12: 3–9.

Elsner, W., and F. S. Lee. (2010). "Editor's Introduction." *American Journal of Economics and Sociology* 69(5): 1333–1344.

Grijalva, T. C., and C. Nowell. (2007). "A Guide to Graduate Study in Economics: Ranking Economics Departments by Fields of Expertise." *Southern Economic Journal* 74(4): 971–996.

Holcombe, R. G. (2004). "The National Research Council Ranking of Research Universities: Its Impact on Research in Economics." *Econ Journal Watch* 1(3): 498–514.

——. (2008). "Pluralism Versus Heterodoxy in Economics and the Social Sciences." *Journal of Philosophical Economics* 1(2): 51–72.

Kapeller, J. (2010). "Citation Metrics: Serious Drawbacks, Perverse Incentives, and Strategic Options for Heterodox Economics." *American Journal of Economics and Sociology* 69(5): 1376–1408.

Klein, D., and E. Chiang. (2004). "The Social Science Citation Index: A Black Box—With an Ideological Bias?" *Econ Journal Watch* 1(1): 134–165.

Klein, D., and C. Stern. (2009). "Groupthink in Academia: Majoritarian Department Politics and the Professional Pyramid." *Independent Review* 13(4): 585–600.

Kohn, M. (2004). "Value and Exchange." *Cato Journal* 24(3): 303–339.

——. (2007). "The Exchange Paradigm: Where to Now?" *Review of Austrian Economics* 20(2/3): 201–203.

Kuhn, T. (1996). *The Structure of Scientific Revolutions.* 3rd ed. Chicago: University of Chicago Press.

Laband, D., and R. D. Tollison. 2000. "On Secondhandism and Scientific Appraisal." *Quarterly Journal of Austrian Economics* 3(1): 43–48.

Lee, F. S. (2007). "The Research Assessment Exercise, the State and the Dominance of Mainstream Economics in British Universities." *Cambridge Journal of Economics* 31: 309–325.

——. (2008). "A Case for Ranking Heterodox Journals and Departments." *On the Horizon* 16(4): 241–251.

Lee, F. S., T. C. Grijalva, and C. Nowell. (2010). "Ranking Economics Departments in a Contested Discipline: A Bibliometric Approach to Quality Equality Between Theoretically Distinct Subdisciplines." *American Journal of Economics and Sociology* 69(5): 1345–1375.

McCloskey, D. M. (1995). "Kelly Green Golf Shoes and the Intellectual Range from M to N." *Eastern Economic Journal* 21(3): 411–414.

Sutter, D. (2007). "Austrian Economics and the Market Test Reconsidered." *Quarterly Journal of Austrian Economics* 10(1): 49–62.

——. (2012). "The Value of Being Different: Doctoral Program Placements of U.S. Heterodox Economics Programs." Unpublished.

Vedder, Richard. (2004). *Going Broke by Degree: Why College Costs So Much.* Washington, DC: American Enterprise Institute.

Chicken Soup for the Out-of-Step Scholar's Soul*

By GENE CALLAHAN† and PETER T. LEESON‡

ABSTRACT. This paper argues that the long-standing predominance of a particular approach to science neither makes it uniquely scientific nor superior to rival approaches. To do so it examines the dominant scientific explanation of the 17th and early 18th centuries: the mechanical philosophy. The mechanical philosophy episode demonstrates the fragility of even the most entrenched scientific wisdoms and provides encouragement for out-of-step scholars everywhere.

> A school of thought is to be viewed as a single individual who talks to himself for a hundred years and is quite extraordinarily pleased with himself, however silly he may be.
>
> —Johann Wolfgang von Goethe ([1821] 1998: 14)

Introduction

As any out-of-step scholar working in the discipline of economics will tell you, the peer-review process sometimes feels more like an exercise in futility for the masochistic than a process that advances economic science. Nearly every academic economist has probably felt this way at least a few times in his career.[1] But besides experiencing this sentiment much more often, the out-of-step scholar experiences the unpleasantness of an unsuccessful attempt to navigate academic peer review in a "special" way.

*We thank Dan Sutter and the participants of the Politics, Philosophy, and Economics workshop at George Mason University for helpful comments on a much earlier draft of this paper. Leeson was the F.A. Hayek Fellow at the London School of Economics at the time of this research and gratefully acknowledges the support of the STICERD Center at the LSE.

†Address: Department of Economics, Purchase College, SUNY, Purchase, NY 10577, USA. Email: eugene.callahan@purchase.edu.

‡Corresponding author. Address: Department of Economics, George Mason University, MS 3G4, Fairfax, VA 22030, USA. Email: PLeeson@GMU.edu.

American Journal of Economics and Sociology, Vol. 71, No. 5 (November, 2012).

The peer-review process tells the unlucky, conventional economist that his paper can't be published because its instrumental variable is invalid and its formal model relies on unjustified assumptions. It tells the unlucky, out-of-step economist that his paper can't be published because it contains neither econometrics nor a formal model. The peer-review process tells the unlucky, conventional economist that his contribution's value added is too small to merit publication. It tells the unlucky, out-of-step economist that his contribution is negative value added: its publication would put economic science back several years—or several centuries. The peer-review process tells the unlucky, conventional economist that his paper has been rejected because its argument has serious flaws. It tells the unlucky, out-of-step economist that his paper has been rejected because it contains no economics.

Faced with repeated rejections of his work on these grounds, the out-of-step economist often feels hopeless. This short article supplies a partial antidote to that sense of hopelessness. We offer a tale of encouragement for the out-of-step scholar. That tale's moral is simple: you needn't be out-of-step, and thus subjected to the peculiar punishments our discipline's refereeing process sometimes subjects you to, forever. There may be a light at the end of your unconventional tunnel.

During the late 17th and early 18th centuries a scientific school called the mechanical philosophy reigned supreme. The core doctrine of the school was that the only valid components of a genuinely scientific explanation comprised the varying extensions, different locations in space, and particular motions of material bodies. Its adherents rejected the notion of a force acting at a distance (for example, gravity, as Newton modeled it, or electro-magnetism, as Maxwell understood it), deeming it an "occult" style of explanation and intrinsically unscientific.

The mechanical philosophers concentrated their research on devising models that purported to capture the essentials of various physical phenomena in nets woven only from their anointed causal factors, showing little concern for whether the abstractions they constructed accurately depicted real entities and processes. When they encountered phenomena that on their surface resisted reduction to mechanical causes, the mechanists invented hypothetical mechanisms to account for them, rendering their system adaptable to otherwise ill-fitting observations or experimental results. After close to a century of enjoying a monopoly on determining what ventures were entitled to the appellation "scientific," the mechanical philosophy lost its preeminence. Today it's a nearly forgotten byway in which science dallied on its journey toward truth.[2]

In what follows the discerning reader will note several similarities between the mechanical philosophy, its devotees' treatment of dissident ideas, and its sway over its discipline, and the dominant approach to economics that pervades the science of economics today. The mechanical philosophy's story reminds us that what most scholars currently see as sensible needn't last forever and that once out-of-step scholars may someday cease to be so.

The Mechanical Philosophy

The story of the mechanical philosophy is unknown to those only familiar with the history of science presented in popular works or scientific textbooks. It's ignored because it doesn't advance the message these accounts hope to convey. Murray Rothbard (1995) called such whitewashing the "Whig history of science," though it might also be called the Voltarian or Enlightenment history of science. In the case of the mechanical philosophy such whitewashing was inspired by the triumphant success of Newtonian mechanics in the 18th century and subsequently advanced by intellectuals eager to propagate this new natural philosophy.

According to the story these intellectuals devised, after the decline of ancient Greek civilization and the rise of Christianity, the project of understanding the world scientifically was abandoned. During the Middle Ages superstition was substituted for science.[3] Only with the work of Copernicus in the 16th century did this trend finally begin to reverse. At the beginning of the 17th century further scientific progress was spearheaded, most notably by Galileo and Kepler. This progress culminated several decades later in the system of understanding the physical world Newton created. Per this account, once religion released science from its stranglehold, science surged ahead along a straight and well-marked road.

The chief obstacle to universal acceptance of this myth was that its tellers had to ignore large parts of the actual history of science to make their story work. Among their significant omissions is the tale of the mechanical philosophy, which dominated scientific theorizing during most of the 17th and the early decades of the 18th centuries. This school of thought, whose members included Descartes, Gassendi, Boyle, Hobbes, and many other notable thinkers, was widely seen as a rational advance over earlier schools of natural philosophy, primarily because it sought to banish all "occult explanations," such as forces acting at a distance or the attribution of any active qualities to matter, from acceptable scientific discourse.

Although the mechanical philosophy took on somewhat different forms in the writings of its various proponents, it can be summarized without too much distortion as being based on the "unfounded ontological reduction of the number of primary qualities to two: 'matter and motion' " (Kuhn 1952: 18). In this reduction matter was forbidden from having any active principles. Descartes, who was perhaps the foremost promoter of mechanism, succinctly stated its guiding principle: "I considered in general all the clear and distinct notions which our understanding can contain with regard to material things. And I found no others except for the notions we have of shapes, sizes and motions" (quoted in Sargent 1995: 32).

In pursuing their research program the mechanical philosophers had a notable enthusiasm for developing models that could account for any phenomenon observed in nature purely on the basis of the size, shape, and motion of particles of matter. However, they paid scant attention to determining whether or not the mechanisms posited by their models really existed. Their focus was on having *some* model that fit their paradigm available for explaining any physical process. Thus "[a] generic kind of corpuscularism, making use of ad hoc postulated particles invented at the whim of the natural philosopher, appears in many texts dating from the middle of the seventeenth century onwards" (Dear 2001: 100).

For instance, the most obvious explanation of magnetism is as an attractive force. But "occult" entities like attractive forces were anathema to the mechanists. To demonstrate that his system could do without such mysterious powers, Descartes devised a mechanical model of magnetic attraction in which the earth and other magnetic bodies emit continual streams of microscopic, screw-shaped particles, which, as they pass through the pores he hypothesized were present in any iron object, draw the iron toward the magnet.

Along the same lines, "[i]n *De Corpore* [Thomas] Hobbes . . . presented a mechanical explanation of the production of cold and ice, both of which he attributed to a 'constant wind' that pressed upon bodies." A liquid freezes when this wind "raises the parts of it in such a way that the uppermost parts become pressed together and thus 'coagulated' " (Sargent 1995: 202–203). Similarly, Robert Boyle and Robert Hooke explained the relationship they discovered between the volume of a certain amount of air and the ambient pressure by "the supposition that air consists of particles like little coiled springs, like wool, which 'consists of many slender and flexible hairs; each of which may indeed, like a little spring, be easily bent and rolled up, but will also, like a spring, be still endeavouring to stretch itself out again' " (Pyle 1995: 476).

Such models will strike those educated in modern science as absurd. But at the time they were put forward the society of respectable, mainstream scholars generally viewed them as representing the most progressive understanding of science, indicating the proper route of advance past the barriers erected by the dogmatic natural philosophy of Aristotle and his Islamic and Scholastic followers. With the benefit of hindsight it's clear that the mechanical philosophy simply replaced Aristotelian restrictions on science with its own, perhaps even more limiting, presuppositions.

The mechanical philosophy's narrow and rigid definition of science automatically dismissed rival approaches as unscientific, stunting the growth of knowledge and derailing scientific inquiry for decades. The subject matter of physics was most amenable to mechanical explanations. However, even here, widespread commitment to strict mechanism had stifling effects in several fields. For instance, "[b]y the end of the 17th century, the mechanical philosophy, which encouraged optics early in the century, and which furnished the idiom in which all students of optics . . . discussed the science, had become an obstacle to further progress." As a result "optics stagnated for a century" (Westfall 1977: 64).

In other sciences the supremacy of the mechanical paradigm was still more obstructive. Westfall (1977: 69) summarizes "the story of chemistry in the second half of the [17th] century [as] the story . . . of its subjection to the mechanical philosophy, since the growing role of mechanisms in chemical literature appears less to have sprung from the phenomena than to have been imposed on them by external considerations."

In lieu of striving to discover the basic, most general causal factors generating the initial appearance of irreducible diversity displayed by chemical phenomena, the mechanical chemists' efforts were chiefly expended in constructing a mechanical model to explain chemical processes constructed using purely mechanical components. "The mechanical philosophy did not in itself offer a chemical theory. On the contrary, it was potentially adaptable to almost any theory" (Westfall 1977: 71).

The mechanist preoccupation with mechanical-based model building, *per se*, was true even of leading chemists of the time, including Nicolas Lemery, the preeminent French chemist of the 17th century. "Like his fellow mechanical chemists, [Lemery] seemed possessed by a mania to explain every property and every phenomenon" in this fashion (Westfall 1977: 73). For example, Lemery's theory of why acids often dissolve metals proposed that the particles composing an acid sport the microscopic equivalent of daggers, which skewer the smooth particles characterizing a metal and then pry the metallic particles apart from their kin. A metal could be precipitated back out of a solution by adding another substance, one whose particles move in such an agitated fashion that they break off the points of those acidic blades, thereby releasing the particles of metal from their captors.

The most prominent, and arguably best, chemist of the 17th century was Robert Boyle. However, "the development of a satisfactory chemical theory as such was not Boyle's goal. Chemistry represented to him a means to demonstrate the validity of the mechanical philosophy of nature" (Westfall 1977: 77). In fact "his mechanical philosophy appears to have operated to thwart the most promising aspect of his chemistry" (Westfall 1977: 79). As Thomas Kuhn (1952: 13) notes, "the form of atomism developed by philosophers and applied to physics in the seventeenth century embraced concepts inconsistent with the development of such fundamental chemical notions as element and compound. These impediments to chemistry are manifest in the chemical theory of . . . Robert Boyle."

According to Westfall (1977: 81), "since there were no criteria by which to judge the superiority of one imagined mechanism over another, the mechanical philosophy itself dissolved into as many versions as there were chemists . . . It is difficult to see that the mechanical philosophy contributed anything to the progress of chemistry as a science." He ends his examination of the chemistry of the period by concluding that "[i]n no area of science was the tendency to imagine invisible mechanisms carried to such extremes" (1977: 81).

The reign of the mechanical philosophy similarly hindered the growth of biological science. It's no coincidence that one of the major biological discoveries made during the period—the recognition that the heart is a pump serving to circulate blood throughout the body—was the achievement not of a mechanical philosopher, but of an animist, William Harvey. Descartes didn't accept Harvey's breakthrough. Instead, he argued that the heart is a sort of heat engine that expands the blood, forcing it to flow through the circulatory system.

The mechanical biologists emphatically rejected the possibility that anything resembling a "formative virtue" could direct the transformation of a fairly simple entity into a much more complex one. When they were confronted with the discovery of mammalian eggs under the microscope, the mechanists hypothesized that a fully formed animal was contained inside each egg. A natural extension of this theory was that if the inhabitant of any egg were a female, then one would find her own eggs inside her. Each of these eggs held one of her fully formed offspring. If female, all these offspring bore the eggs of the generation to follow theirs, and so on. Thus it appeared quite likely "that the entire human race was present already in Eve" (Westfall 1977: 100). The most obvious alternative explanation of the discovery in question views an embryo as developing in stages of successive differentiation. This view suggests the operation of "occult organizing forces . . . but the mid-eighteenth century, with its strong preference for the mechanical ideas set forth by Descartes . . . was not the ideal time to propose intangible driving impulses" (Pinto-Correia 1997: 171).

Mechanistic biological theories like those described above were not formulated based on mechanical philosophers' critical examination of biological phenomena. Before even turning their attention to the concrete realities with which the world of living creatures confronted them, they had already concluded that *only* mechanical explanations qualified as truly scientific. Consequently, their theorizing revolved around figuring out how to squeeze the embarrassment of unwieldy and complex patterns exhibited by living processes into their self-limited choice of pre-formed moulds. "[Mechanistic biology] did not arise from the demands of biological study; it was far more the puppet regime set up by the mechanical philosophy's invasion" (Westfall 1977: 104).

The mechanical philosophy gradually lost its authority over matters involving scientific legitimacy during the first half of the 18th century. Its decline can be attributed primarily to two factors: the increasingly apparent arbitrariness and complexity of the models it offered and the recognition of the tremendous explanatory economy of Newton's distinctly non-mechanical theory of gravity. The inequality of the contest between mechanism and Newtonianism was manifest in mechanical philosophers' attempts to develop a plausible gravitational model of their own that could compete with Newton's. This project led them to propose obviously unworkable theories in which all celestial bodies were held to be surrounded by vortices of "subtle matter," which somehow drove objects composed of grosser matter down towards the body from all directions at once.

Based largely on its founder's country of birth, Newtonianism most rapidly supplanted the mechanical philosophy in Great Britain where the former was the clear victor by the beginning of the century. In contrast, the mechanical philosophy held sway in France until roughly mid-century when Voltaire's vigorous advocacy of Newton's system finally overcame the clout of the country's native son, Descartes. Thus it took time for Newton's theory to gradually gain acceptance outside his homeland and permeate the scientific attitudes of those in surrounding areas.

Importantly, during this shift in the dominant scientific paradigm, science sometimes moved forward by going "backward" to concepts the mechanical philosophers had previously rejected as unscientific. For instance, Newton's theory of gravity implied that one material body was somehow able to affect another one without the pair having any direct physical contact. On publishing his ideas, the Cartesians widely derided Newton for forwarding "manifest stupidity" (Pinto-Correia 1997: 171). Mainstream scholars saw his theory as a regression into murky and unintelligible terrain haunted by the "occult forces" Renaissance naturalism posited.

Newton frankly claimed the very reversion to antique theories his critics held against him as a virtue. He attributed his success in advancing mathematics to having launched his explorations from a careful study of the ancient Greek geometers. Newton rejected the idea that his advances proceeded from the contemporary ideas of Cartesian analytical geometry, which he described as "the Analysis of the Bunglers in Mathematicks" (Westfall 1980: 379–380).

Furthermore, several unconventional theories proposed during the reign of the mechanical philosophy, theories then rejected as unworthy of serious consideration by the scientific mainstream, were eventually resuscitated in the wake of the mechanical philosophy's demise. Consider, again, Newton. Newton's conjecture that all material bodies are composed of only a very few elementary particles, and that what appear to be chemical elements are really compounds of those building blocks, and, therefore, could be transformed into each other, was seen as an unsightly blemish on his great career for two centuries.

However, as Pyle (1995: 433) notes, "[t]his criticism seems unfair and unwarranted. In the first place, the Newtonian matter-theory is remarkably close to what we now believe to be the truth. Chemical species do only arise at a 'molecular' level, that is as a result of the aggregation of simpler (and chemical neutral) constituents. The chemical atom of Dalton is a highly complex structure, made up of neutrons, protons, and electrons, held together by powerful interparticulate forces of various kinds. The transmutation of the so-called 'chemical elements' is physically possible although, as Newton foresaw, highly difficult owing to the strength of those forces."

Concluding Remarks

The tale of the mechanical philosophy should provide some comfort to out-of-step economists who confront the challenges this paper began with. This tale demonstrates the fragility of even the most entrenched scientific "wisdoms" and suggests that once-derided approaches to understanding the world can come to displace currently fashionable approaches even when such displacement appears impossible.

However, the process that can lead to such displacement isn't inevitable. It requires out-of-step scholars to continue their out-of-step work. Unconventional researchers must not placidly drift with the prevalent scientific tide like so many jellyfish bobbing in the waves. If Newton had taken this attitude, we might still be stuck with the mechanical philosophy. The greatest scientists have often been the ones who had the courage to swim against the current of their time. There's no reason to think economics is an exception in this regard.

Two lessons from the rise and decline of the mechanical philosophy are especially important for out-of-step scholars to keep in mind as they search for energy to continue being out-of-step. First, it's not the case that a real science must forget its forefathers. Sometimes, the impetus needed to surmount some barrier blocking progress can be provided by the ideas of a long-dead thinker. This was partly the case with Newton, whose ideas finally triumphed over the mechanical philosophy, and could very well be the case in economics as well.

Under the weight of popular scientific preconceptions in the economics profession, the field of history of economic thought is quickly dying. Only a rapidly shrinking number of departments offer courses in the subject. There are only a handful of jobs available in history of thought each year. And the field is generally looked down on by the rest of the economics profession. This is unfortunate. But those who have retained their interest—a group in economics whose membership overlaps significantly with those seen as out-of-step more generally—should forge ahead, as they may be in the best position to contribute to the advance of economic knowledge in the long run.

Second, and perhaps most important, it's not the case that science always makes steady progress. Science sometimes enters cul-de-sacs that it must eventually back out of in order to move forward again. Although the mechanical philosophers' monopoly on science stunted advances in knowledge, it was ultimately dislodged and, free from its fetters, science again was able to progress. If out-of-step scholars are willing to continue their work, there is no reason this couldn't also happen in economics, no matter how dim the chances appear at present.

Notes

1. This is true even of those who have made some of the most important contributions to economics. See, for instance, Gans and Shepherd (1994).

2. Various episodes in more recent scientific history, such as Einstein explaining gravity as a curvature in space instead of as a force acting at a distance, could reasonably be viewed as a revival of the type of theory favored by the mechanical philosophy. But we aren't making any metaphysical claims about the ultimate status of mechanical explanations. Our argument is historical: the mechanical philosophy didn't provide the framework needed to make progress in a number of fields and in fact stifled progress in several fields within the context of its time.

3. See Grant (1996) against this view.

References

Dear, P. (2001). *Revolutionizing the Sciences: European Knowledge and its Ambitions, 1500–1700.* Houndsmills: Palgrave.

Gans, J. S., and G. B. Shepherd. (1994). "How Are the Mighty Fallen: Rejected Classic Articles by Leading Economists." *Journal of Economic Perspectives* 8(1): 165–179.

Goethe, J. W. von. ([1821] 1998). *Maxims and Reflections.* London: Penguin Books.

Grant, E. (1996). *The Foundations of Modern Science in the Middle Ages.* Cambridge: Cambridge University Press.

Kuhn, T. S. (1952). "Robert Boyle and Structural Chemistry in the Seventeenth Century." *Isis* 43(1): 12–36.

Pinto-Correia, C. (1997). *The Ovary of Eve.* Chicago: University of Chicago Press.

Pyle, A. (1995). *Atomism and its Critics: From Democritus to Newton.* Bristol: Thoemmes Press.

Rothbard, M. N. (1995). *An Austrian Perspective on the History of Economic Thought.* Aldershot: Edward Elgar.

Sargent, R.-M. (1995). *The Diffident Naturalist: Robert Boyle and the Philosophy of Experiment.* Chicago: University of Chicago Press.

Westfall, R. S. (1977). *The Construction of Modern Science: Mechanisms and Mechanics.* Cambridge: Cambridge University Press.

——. (1980). *Never at Rest: A Biography of Isaac Newton.* Cambridge: Cambridge University Press

Beyond Kelly Green Golf Shoes: Evaluating the Demand for Scholarship of Free-Market and Mainstream Economists

By J. R. CLARK#, JENNIFER MILLER-WILFORD*, and EDWARD PETER STRINGHAM†

ABSTRACT. We evaluate statistics from the Social Science Research Network (SSRN) to see how much free-market economists are being read and ranked compared with mainstream economists. We find that under various rankings using SSRN data, the top free-market economists rank among the most-read authors in the economics profession.

Introduction

In asking the question of James Buchanan (1964), "What should economists do?" McCloskey (1995: 411) argues that the economics profession has become overly narrow and is producing too much of a product demanded by few: "Shoemaker, stick to your last" is good advice only if the shoemaker makes shoes that people want to buy. But if he's piling up kelly green golfing shoes with chartreuse tassels in his back yard unsold, or more exactly "sold" only to other shoemakers, the advice is bad. It's the advice a specialized economist has been following for some time. Producers of kelly green golf shoes may impress each other with their work, but without measures of how much non-producers actually value their work, how can we determine if an economist is producing something of value?

Various criteria of achievement or output exist in the economics profession, but whether they measure demand is unclear. One common measure is the length of one's curriculum vitae and augmented measures attempt to give more weight to higher-ranked journals. But just because a writer produces a lot of work (even in top-ranked journals) does not mean that many readers see much value in those articles. In this case, sometimes supply does not create

#University of Tennessee at Chattanooga, *Arizona State University, †Fayetteville State University, probasco@utc.edu, jwilford@asu.edu, estringh@uncfsu.edu.

American Journal of Economics and Sociology, Vol. 71, No. 5 (November, 2012).

demand. After an article gets through the referee process, how many people actually read it? One could say that acceptances indicate that editors are demanding the articles, but it seems that such a measurement of demand is limited.[1]

Of the economics profession, Thoma writes to *The Economist* (2011), "Nobody reads the journals themselves much anymore"; he states that publishing in economics journals is about establishing a pecking order.

Another way to measure demand is by looking at citations, a quantifiable yet often nebulous tool because this too may fall prey to the kelly green golf shoes problem. The Social Science Citation Impact (SSCI), for example, measures not how much one is cited overall or cited in economics journals, but instead citations from SSCI-listed journals to other SSCI-listed journals.[2] Holcombe (2004), Klein and Chiang (2004), and Lee et al. (2010) point out that the SSCI is quite insular and leaves out most journals outside the mainstream—or what McCloskey (1995: 411) would refer to as the "[i]ntellectual range from N to M."[3] If a measure picks up only kelly green golf shoes, then it misses whether anyone but producers of kelly green golf shoes value a product.

In this article we examine an alternative measure of demand for economic research based on downloads and other statistics from an online article repository, the Social Science Research Network (SSRN). SSRN allows journals and authors to upload articles for others to download. In addition to showing how many articles an author has written, the website provides data on many other statistics, including how much each article is downloaded. Many academics use SSRN to rank individuals, departments, and schools. At Harvard, for example, they declare, "Harvard corporate faculty lead SSRN rankings" (Hirst 2011). *The New York Times* (Cohen 2008) published an article about SSRN rankings titled, "Now professors get their star rankings, too," and academics including Brown (2003) and Black and Caron (2006) have discussed the benefits of using SSRN rankings.

A key advantage of SSRN rankings is that they count not only how much work an academic produces, but also how many people demand to read that author's work. In *The New York Times* article about SSRN (Cohen 2008), Cass Sunstein said: "The gatekeepers matter, but don't have the enormous power to deny people a large audience." One way to leave the ranking to the readers is to look at how much readers actually download an author's articles. SSRN's main ranking focuses on total downloads in the past year, but SSRN provides data and lets one rank authors in various ways such as downloads per article or all-time downloads.

Analysis of the SSRN data results in some predictable and other less predictable findings. The top 100 authors or top 100 authors in economics departments in SSRN's main ranking, which focuses on total new downloads, includes many famous economists from institutions such as MIT and Harvard, including Daron Acemoglu, Olivier Blanchard, Edward Glaeser, Michael Jensen, and Andrei Shleifer. This first category of mainstream economists publishes a lot and is read a lot. Further down in the SSRN rankings is a second category of mainstream economists who publish a lot but are not downloaded a lot. People may read these authors' work in outlets other than SSRN and thus the SSRN data are not showing the complete picture. However, many of these scholars simply may be very good at producing kelly green golf shoes that they like, but much less good at producing articles that more than a handful of people actually read.

How free-market economists (including many associated with the Austrian school of economics) compare with the mainstream is most interesting. Rosen (1997) and Laband and Tollison (2000) have criticized Austrians for not passing the market test. Similar charges are often lodged against free-market economists more generally. When analyzing actual data from SSRN, however, a different picture emerges. This article looks at how free-market economists fare in SSRN rankings compared with mainstream scholars and finds that the top free-market economists and top Austrian economists rank very favorably. For example, according to SSRN's main ranking, Peter Boettke ranks in the top 100 of all 100,000+ authors on SSRN and in the top 10 of all 10,000+ authors in economics departments worldwide. Looking at individual categories that SSRN ranks, the top 25 free-market economists on our list consistently rank in the top 5 percent of all scholars on SSRN. Rather than producing articles that show academic prowess and are read by few, the top free-market economists and top Austrian economists produce articles that people actually want to read.

Data

The main data set collected in this article is from SSRN from October 2011. Let us summarize how SSRN works and how people use it, and then discuss how free-market economists fare in the rankings. SSRN is an Internet repository to which journals and individual scholars can upload copies of working papers or published works. Some journals automatically upload articles, but scholars are welcome to upload articles published in any journal. Economics is the most popular discipline on SSRN, followed by law and business-related disciplines. As of this writing, SSRN included more than 300,000 articles that have been downloaded a total of almost 50 million times (see Tables 1 and 2). Because SSRN has so many articles that can be downloaded for free, it has become quite popular. SSRN has partnered with hundreds of publishers and is positively mentioned in outlets ranging from *Encyclopedia Britannica* to *USA Today* (Hannon 2010).

Anyone who signs up for a free account with SSRN can look at these rankings. SSRN provides data on each article, author, and department,

Table 1

Summary Article and Usage Statistics of SSRN

Combined eLibrary Networks	
Abstracts	345,877
Full Text Papers	281,086
Authors	163,653
Downloads to Date	45,912,763
Downloads in Last 12 Months	8,646,426
Downloads in Last 30 Days	648,235
Total References	6,883,617
Total Citation Links	4,446,080
Total Footnotes	7,169,444

Table 2

Summary of Articles in SSRN by Discipline

Network	Papers in eLibrary
Accounting Research	15,883
Cognitive Science	4,534
Corporate Governance	12,158
Economics Research	221,960
Entrepreneurship Research and Policy	18,316
Financial Economics	85,721
Health Economics	5,242
Information Systems and eBusiness	9,088
Legal Scholarship	112,228
Management Research	34,397
Political Science	30,427
Social Insurance Research	5,088
Humanities	17,620

and it updates the data daily, weekly, or monthly depending on the statistic. SSRN collects data on and ranks authors by new and all-time papers uploaded, new[4] and all-time download for all papers, new and all-time downloads per paper, total citations, and citations per paper. Citations are measured by how many other works in SSRN cite a particular work on SSRN. This measure faces a similar problem as the SSCI measure citations, which only looks at citations in SSCI journals to other SSCI listed journals. On the other hand, because SSRN does not have the same SSCI gatekeeper issue where only certain SSCI journals qualify, any citation counts as long as any article in SSRN cites it. This will not have the same bias against heterodox scholars whose journals are not approved by someone like the SSCI gatekeeper, although if heterodox scholars tend to be cited by heterodox scholars and their numbers are fewer they will still have fewer citations even with this expanded measure. SSRN also presents a more complicated weighted measure of citations, the Eigenfactor score.[5] In addition to compiling data on individuals, SSRN aggregates scholars into departments or schools so that one can rank institutions.

We do not have a strong opinion on which among SSRN's potential rankings is best, although we see advantages to SSRN's main ranking based on total new downloads, so we sort our tables and highlight the rankings based on that. SSRN's main ranking that focuses on total new downloads can be viewed as important for the following reasons. While all-time past achievements matter, so does current demand. For example, although Brett Favre has the most passing yards in National Football League history, in 2008 the Green Bay Packers were almost certainly right to look at the current and likely future productivity of their 38-year-old quarterback's replacement (a 24 year old who won them the Super Bowl within three years). Similarly, in 2008 lenders considering giving loans to General Motors were correct to focus not on all-time auto sales but instead on statistics about current and expected future sales when determining whether General Motors was likely to repay its loans.

It is important to highlight some qualifiers about the data, and we will repeat some of these points more than once lest they be missed. We do not make the claim that SSRN rankings measure someone's work as "better," "more interesting," or "more influential," or because someone is more popular they are a better scholar. Even if more people read an economist's articles, that does not mean that the readers gain from the articles or even like them. Some downloads may be in-depth reads whereas others might involve casual glances or even disgust never to think of it again. Next, SSRN's main ranking that focuses on total new downloads may be an important measure of current demand (akin to this year's, as opposed to lifetime, statistics in sports), but, of course, it would be just as fallacious to conclude that this year's most-downloaded economist is a better economist than Adam Smith as it would to say that this year's home run king is a better all-time player than Babe Ruth. What's more, SSRN has data only for the 100,000+ scholars registered with its system so it only ranks those registered in the database. For example, Adam Smith wrote at a time when SSRN.com was not widely available, so he is not included in current SSRN rankings. Many living scholars, typically those closer to retirement age, probably have more important things to do with their time than register in online databases, so many great economists like Roger Garrison, Thomas Sowell, or Leland Yeager are not included on the list. So the SSRN data only allow comparisons between scholars who are on the system.

Finally, one obviously must use caution when looking at particular statistics in isolation to avoid concluding that a home run king with a low batting average and few runs batted in is the best or most valuable player overall. As contributors to the field of sabermetrics pointed out, some people focus on highly visible statistics like home runs while ignoring other important statistics like number of walks. Such a point does not dismiss the data, it simply says one should be careful what to emphasize. The data presented in this article could be easily sorted differently, averaged, or weighted to create other measures. For example, in the final two columns of Tables 3 and 4 we created two new composite scores, one that averages each author's rankings across all categories and a second that averages each author's percentiles across all categories. In addition, one could create other rankings that put some weight on SSRN data and other weight on completely different data such as SSCI. Our Excel files also included the data and rankings from Sutter (2012), but space limits how much we can display. If we had 10 times as much space we would show the tables sorted in 10 ways, but instead of doing that we will focus on SSRN's main ranking that focuses on total new downloads and simply mention some of the other sorting options in the text.

With these qualifiers in mind, we still believe that looking at metrics such as current home runs or downloads on SSRN does provide some important and useful information. When an economist is widely downloaded we doubt that all of the downloads are accidental. The data at least allows us to see whom readers do or do not pay attention to on SSRN.

Here our interest is specifically how free-market economists compare with economists in the rest of the profession. One can debate how to classify someone as a free-market economist, and we think such a debate is useful. For the purposes of this article, however, we began with Sutter's (2012) roughly 400-person list of free-market economists and selected those who published in or served on the editorial board of one of six free-market journals in the five years prior to Sutter's study. A few economists on this list, such as David Colander or Sandra Peart, likely would not classify themselves as free market, but they do publish in or on editorial boards of free-market outlets, so, like Sutter, we include them on our list. Our ranking is also limited to scholars listed on SSRN (among the top 50 free-market economists in Sutter's ranking, 40 are listed on SSRN).[6]

Table 3 presents data for the top 25 free-market economists ranked according to SSRN's main ranking that focuses on total new downloads (we will refer to this as SSRN's main ranking). The table also displays rankings in other individual categories that could be used to sort the table. For each category, SSRN provides the raw score used to create a ranking, the specific rank among all authors on SSRN, and we calculate a percentile ranking among all authors on SSRN. SSRN lists 117,095 Total Authors in its system and 11,604 Authors in Economics Departments.[7] Rather than comparing the free-market economists to the 11,604 Authors in Economics Departments, we choose to compare them to All Authors in the system because many economists (for example, Eugene Fama, Richard Thaler, Kevin Murphy [none of whom are on Sutter's or our list of free market economists]) teach in business schools and are listed in SSRN as Authors in Business Schools.

According to SSRN's main ranking, Peter Boettke is 84th out of 117,095 Authors in SSRN, which puts him in the top one tenth of 1 percent. If we were to narrow the ranking to only scholars in Economics Departments (these data are not presented in Table 3), Boettke is 9th out of 11,604 scholars. If Peter Boettke ever encounters a protestor from the 2011–2012 Occupy Wall Street movement, he can tell them that he is not just part of the One Percent but part of the top 1/10 of the One Percent. Other free-market economists also rank quite highly: Edward Stringham and Philip Graves rank in the top 500 (top 1/2 of 1 percent) and Stan Leibowitz, Peter Klein, and Christopher Coyne rank in the Top 1,000 (top 1 percent). In SSRN's main ranking, all top 25 free-market economists rank among the top 5 percent of all authors in SSRN. In addition, Table 3 presents data for individual rankings such as the Eigenfactor score. Looking at Eigenfactor score or the composite ranking equally weighted across all categories, Peter Boettke, Edward Stringham, Philip Graves, Stan Leibowitz, Peter Klein, and Christopher Coyne all rank within the top 5 percent of all authors.[8]

Table 3

Top-Ranked Free-Market Economists Using SSRN Rankings

SSRN Main Ranking of Free-Market Economists	**Name**	University	Total New Downloads	**Total New Downloads Rank**	# of New Papers	**# of New Papers Rank**	New Downloads per Paper	**New Downloads Per Paper Rank**	All Time Downloads	**All Time Downloads Rank**	Citations	**Citations Rank**	# of Total Papers	**# of Papers Rank**	Downloads per Paper	**Downloads Per Raper Rank**	Citations per Paper	**Citations Per Paper Rank**	Eigenfactor Score (x100)	**Eigenfactor Rank**	Composite Rank Equally Weighted Across All Categories	Composite Percentile Equally Rated Across All Categories
1	**Boettke, Peter**	GMU	7,139	84***	35	25***	45	4,768**	9,569	1,190**	196	2,227**	160	28***	60	17,345	1	12,500	0.92	1,815**	4,442**	3.6
2	**Stringham, Ed**	Fayetteville	2,801	473***	7	1,013***	72	2,314**	3,710	4,263**	70	5,333**	39	1,026***	95	13,084	2	9,511*	0.28	4,770**	4,643**	3.5
3	**Graves, Philip**	Colorado	2,740	490***	15	197***	39	5,671**	4,427	3,425**	147	2,870**	70	270***	63	16,883	2	9,511*	0.41	3,490**	4,756**	3.7
4	**Liebowitz, Stan**	UT Dallas	2,280	659***	5	1,956**	62	2,960**	19,420	388***	215	2,023**	37	1,136**	525	1,478**	6	4,377**	1.33	1,322**	1,811**	1.4
5	**Klein, Peter**	Missouri	2,162	729***	4	2,908**	62	2,960**	16,179	517***	228	1,910**	35	1,268**	462	1,866**	7	3,736**	0.78	2,083**	1,997**	1.5
6	**Coyne, Chris**	GMU	2,106	758***	16	169***	44	4,901**	2,717	6,024*	79	4,829**	48	689***	57	17,778	2	9,511*	0.28	4,655**	5,479*	4.2
7	**Carden, W. Art**	Rhodes	1,374	1,503**	2	7,957*	35	6,488*	5,715	2,433**	30	9,944*	39	1,026***	147	8,970*	1	12,500	0.04	17,178	7,555*	4.8
8	**Smith, Vernon**	Chapman	1,358	1,528**	2	7,957*	47	4,449**	12,950	768***	83	4,643**	29	1,847**	447	1,981**	3	7,551*	0.22	5,703**	4,047**	2.9
9	**Rubin, Paul**	Emory	1,242	1,733**	7	1,013***	26	8,858*	14,799	601***	206	2,101**	48	689***	308	3,665**	4	6,144*	1.25	1,400**	2,912**	2.4
10	**Stratmann, Thomas**	GMU	1,032	2,234**	2	7,957**	23	9,911*	8,183	1,483**	143	2,935**	44	807***	186	7,016*	3	7,551*	0.51	2,942**	4,760**	3.8
11	**Selgin, George**	Georgia	1,020	2,268**	1	16,321	340		1,167	13,996	2	39,611	3	32,168	389		1			61,539	27,651	9.9
12	**Leeson, Peter**	GMU	1,006	2,302**	8	767***	37	6,086*	1,188	13,790	60	6,007*	27	2,129**	44	19,794	2	9,511*	0.17	6,716*	7,456*	5.7
13	**Hoover, Kevin**	Duke	1,001	2,314**	4	2,908**	36	6,303*	5,182	2,791**	95	4,160**	28	1,974**	185	7,068*	3	7,551*	0.43	3,370**	4,271**	3.3
14	**Peart, Sandra**	Richmond	983	2,378**	1	16,321	66	2,674**	3,491	4,581**	15	15,452	15	5,765**	233	5,342**	1	12,500	0.04	15,660	8,964*	6.2
15	**Margolis, Stephen**	NC State	925	2,601**	2	7,957**	132	654***	4,640	3,250**	83	4,643**	7	15,093	663	930***	12	2,062**	0.38	3,693**	4,543**	3.5
16	**Horwitz, Steven**	St. Lawrence	890	2,751**	5	1,956**	81	1,804**	1,027	15,728	1	47,872	11	8,868*	93	13,321	0	17,528	0.00	44,201	17,114	10.4
17	**Storr, Virgil**	GMU	881	2,794**	19	120***	37	6,086*	1,018	15,853	33	9,361*	24	2,657**	42	20,096	1	12,500	0.11	9,085*	8,728*	6.6
18	**Sautet, Frederic**	Mercatus	787	3,232**	3	4,545**	36	6,303*	1,885	8,908*	14	16,102	22	3,117**	86	14,043	1	12,500	0.03	20,828	9,953*	6.5
19	**Congleton, Roger**	WVU	755	3,435**	6	1,387**	20	11,101*	4,434	34,228	44	7,623**	37	1,136**	120	10,817*	1	12,500	0.13	7,916*	6,593*	4.9
20	**Colander, David**	Middlebury	739	3,547**	3	4,545**	92	1,428**	1,782	9,411*	17	14,279	8	13,050	223	5,645**	2	9,511*	0.05	15,164	8,509*	5.8
21	**Kuran, Timur**	Duke	713	3,703**	1	16,321	59	3,209**	7,796	1,593**	80	4,778**	12	7,940*	650	973*	7	3,736**	0.80	2,052**	4,923**	4.0
22	**Klein, Daniel**	GMU	641	4,251**	5	1,956**	12	15,522	4,746	3,154**	71	5,269**	52	568***	91	13,510	1	12,500	0.49	3,002**	6,637*	5.4
23	**Meiners, Roger**	UT Arlington	564	4,975**	0	49,637	113	912***	4,488	3,376**	5	27,598	5	20,998	898	466***	1	12,500	0.02	24,736	16,133	11.4
24	**Lipecap, Gary**	UC SB	557	5,067**	8	767***	11	16,199	4,647	3,246**	161	2,649**	49	653***	95	13,084	3	7,551*	0.65	2,405**	5,736*	4.7
25	**Kroszner, Randall**	Chicago	557	5,067**	1	16,321	19	11,542*	8,055	1,515**	680	574***	29	1,847**	278	4,224**	23	781***	2.28	787***	4,740**	4.0

To put these data into perspective, Table 4 compares the top six free-market economists to some other well-known mainstream economists. Rather than simply presenting a long list of the top 5,000 authors on SSRN, which includes many non-economists, we select some recognized economists who clearly have registered and are active users of SSRN (our cutoff is 20 or more articles uploaded). Some predictable and perhaps less predictable results emerge. The highest-rated scholar, Michael Jensen, and the top mainstream economists right behind him rank well in all categories. Using a composite rank equally weighted across all categories the top economists include Michael Jensen, Olivier Blanchard, Andrei Shleifer, Ross Levine, and Nicholas Economides. Sorting individually by the Eigenfactor score or total number of downloads, one sees other well-known economists, Steven Shavell, Edward Glaeser, Raghuram Rajan, and Daron Acemoglu, ranking highly, which is unsurprising because they, after all, are well-known economists. How the top free-market economists fare compared to the top mainstream scholars is noteworthy. On the basis of SSRN's main ranking, Peter Boettke ranks ahead of big names including Kevin Murphy, Luigi Zingales, and Rafael la Porta. After Boettke, Edward Stringham, Philip Graves, Stan Leibowitz, Peter Klein, and Christopher Coyne also rank ahead of many famous economists, including Esther Duflo, Elinor Ostrom, Kenneth Rogoff, and William Easterly. Again, these rankings do not indicate who is a better economist, but instead what economists are more downloaded in recent times. Looking at the composite ranking that averages one's percentile in each category, Stan Leibowitz, Peter Klein, Peter Boettke, Edward Stringham, Philip Graves, and Christopher Coyne have an average percentile across all categories within the top 5 percent ahead of well-known economists including Meckling, Landes, and Fischel for that composite average.

In her sociological analysis of the economics profession, Copp (1992) writes: "Small organized coherent groups have consistently been associated with major scientific changes. This relationship occurs in a variety of disciplines and over long periods of time." George Mason University, in particular, is home to 30 free-market economists who appear on our master list, and 7 of these are in the top 25 free-market economists. Let us consider how they compare to other

Table 4

Comparing Top-Ranked Free-Market Economists to Select Top-Ranked Mainstream Economists Using SSRN Rankings

SSRN Main Ranking of All Authors in SSRN	Name	University	Total New Downloads	Total New Downloads Rank	# of New Papers	# of New Papers Rank	New Downloads per Paper	New Downloads Per Paper Rank	All Time Downloads	All Time Downloads Rank	Citations	Citations Rank	# of Total Papers	# of Papers Rank	Downloads per Paper	Downloads Per Raper Rank	Citations per Paper	Citations Per Paper Rank	Eigenfactor Score (x100)	Eigenfactor Rank	Composite Rank Equally Weighted Across All Categories	Composite Percentile Equally
1	Jensen, Michael	Harvard	71,102	1***	6	1,387**	603	32***	533,954	1***	12,265	2***	118	61***	4,525	13***	104	26***	81.33	1***	169***	0.1
84	*Boettke, Peter*	*GMU*	*7,139*	*84****	*35*	*25****	*45*	*4,768***	*9,569*	*1,190***	*196*	*2,227***	*160*	*28****	*60*	*17,345*	*1*	*12,500*	*0.92*	*1,815***	*4,442***	*3.6*
86	Murphy, Kevin	USC	7,005	86***	3	4,545**	250	182***	70,064	38***	3,841	35***	28	1,974**	2,502	47***	137	12***	28.63	18***	771***	0.7
191	Zingales, Luigi	Chicago	4,632	191***	6	1,387**	35	6,488*	58,042	49***	6,117	9***	132	46***	440	2,049**	46	185***	29.57	16***	1,158**	1.0
292	Acemoglu, Daron	MIT	3,672	292***	29	43***	17	12,524	25,228	256***	5,566	13***	211	5***	120	10,817*	26	629***	33.01	9***	2,732**	2.3
293	Lopez de Silanes, Florencio	EDHEC	3,668	293***	1	16,321	60	3,138**	44,573	73***	9,530	5***	61	379***	731	742***	156	9***	27.24	23***	2,331**	2.0
456	La Porta, Rafael	Dartmouth	2,867	456***	2	7,957*	53	3,741**	38,779	103***	9,554	4***	54	530***	718	772***	177	4***	26.23	26***	1,510**	1.3
457	Glaeser, Edward	Harvard	2,864	457***	9	585***	14	14,216	40,779	92***	5,040	16***	198	9***	206	6,222*	25	678***	34.83	6***	2,476**	2.1
485	Shavell, Steven	Harvard	2,748	485***	3	4,545**	24	9,549*	34,551	137***	3,106	48***	115	70***	300	3,802**	27	589***	35.54	5***	2,137**	1.8
473	*Stringham, Edward*	*Fayetteville*	*2,801*	*473****	*7*	*1,013****	*72*	*2,314***	*3,710*	*4,263***	*70*	*5,333***	*39*	*1,026****	*95*	*13,084*	*2*	*9,511**	*0.28*	*4,770***	*4,643***	*3.5*
490	*Graves, Philip*	*Colorado*	*2,740*	*490****	*15*	*197****	*39*	*5,671***	*4,427*	*3,425***	*147*	*2,870***	*70*	*270****	*63*	*16,883*	*2*	*9,511**	*0.41*	*3,490***	*4,756***	*3.7*
556	Rajan, Raghuram	Chicago	2,522	556***	8	767***	27	8,543*	37,388	114***	5,765	12***	95	121***	394	2,501**	61	93***	31.63	11***	1,413**	1.2
565	Epstein, Richard	NYU	2,487	565***	5	1,956**	46	4,601**	16,454	506***	53	6,627*	54	530***	305	3,704**	1	12,500	0.21	5,726**	4,079**	2.9
627	Viscusi, W. Kip	Vanderbilt	2,339	627***	17	151***	21	10,685	17,046	473***	533	760***	109	85***	156	8,447*	5	5,137**	5.00	334***	2,966**	2.5
632	Hoxby, Caroline	Stanford	2,331	632***	1	16,321	80	1,854**	44,830	71***	573	701***	29	1,847**	1,546	137***	20	991***	7.16	219***	2,530**	2.1
634	Posner, Richard	Chicago	2,330	634***	0	49,637	63	2,889**	33,163	151***	598	671***	37	1,136**	896	469***	16	1,369**	6.34	253***	6,357*	5.4
659	*Liebowitz, Stan*	*UT—Dallas*	*2,280*	*659****	*5*	*1,956***	*62*	*2,960***	*19,420*	*388****	*215*	*2,023***	*37*	*1,136***	*525*	*1,478***	*6*	*4,377***	*1.33*	*1,322***	*1,811***	*1.4*
729	*Klein, Peter*	*Missouri*	*2,162*	*729****	*4*	*2,908***	*62*	*2,960***	*16,179*	*517****	*228*	*1,910***	*35*	*1,268***	*462*	*1,866***	*7*	*3,736***	*0.78*	*2,083***	*1,997***	*1.5*
758	*Coyne, Christopher*	*GMU*	*2,106*	*758****	*16*	*169****	*44*	*4,901***	*2,717*	*6,024**	*79*	*4,829***	*48*	*689****	*57*	*17,778*	*2*	*9,511**	*0.28*	*4,655***	*5,479**	*4.2*
910	Duflo, Esther	MIT	1,886	910***	5	1,956**	27	8,543*	12,996	763***	1,784	136***	70	270***	186	7,016*	25	678***	13.09	85***	2,262**	1.9
928	Ostrom, Elinor	Indiana	1,858	928***	8	767***	62	2,960**	6,264	2,185**	26	10,995*	30	1,716**	209	6,104*	1	12,500	0.14	7,775*	5,103*	3.6
969	Eichengreen, Barry	Berkeley	1,808	969***	19	120***	12	15,522	10,884	987***	2,067	110***	149	35***	73	15,560	14	1,659**	9.88	136***	3,900**	3.3
1024	Rogoff, Kenneth	Harvard	1,756	1,024***	12	334***	21	10,685*	10,551	1,032***	4,087	28***	82	176***	129	10,140*	50	154***	19.04	48***	2,625**	2.2
1025	Landes, William	Chicago	1,753	1,025***	0	49,637	83	1,733**	69,595	40***	202	2,158**	21	3,386**	3,314	28***	10	2,541**	1.55	1,159***	6,856*	5.7
1126	Easterly, William	NYU	1,657	1,126**	2	7,957*	26	8,858*	14,542	623***	2,121	108***	63	355***	231	5,405**	34	366***	9.41	148***	2,772**	2.4
1195	Weingast, Barry	Stanford	1,592	1,195**	3	4,545**	69	2,484**	5,118	2,841**	182	2,377**	23	2,878**	223	5,645**	8	3,245**	0.49	3,014**	3,136**	2.4

mainstream economics departments or business schools. The top 10 lists of economics departments and of business schools include the institutions one would expect. The top U.S. economics departments in SSRN's main ranking are Harvard, Cornell, Massachusetts Institute of Technology (MIT), New York University (NYU), and Princeton (see Table 5), and the top U.S. business schools in SSRN's main ranking are Harvard, NYU, University of Chicago, University of Pennsylvania, and MIT. These rankings are quite consistent with those from *U.S. News and World Report* or *EconPhD.net*, which include all of the above schools in their top 25. How does the largely free-market department at George Mason University compare? In SSRN's main ranking of economics departments worldwide, George Mason University is 8th in the U.S. (and 13th in the world), just behind Berkeley (6th in the U.S. and 10th worldwide) and Brown (7th in the U.S. and 12th worldwide) and ahead of many heavyweights, including Duke and Stanford.[9] Again, whether the economics practiced at George Mason University is "better" or "more interesting" than that practiced at the lower-ranked institutions is a subjective question. But the fact is that more people are currently downloading research from George Mason University free-market economists than from all but 12 other departments in the world.

Conclusion

Many free-market economists rank quite highly in SSRN compared with their peers in the mainstream. An advantage of the SSRN data is they show how much an author is actually downloaded rather than how much he is published or where. The measurement does not depend on gatekeepers or existing practices of the profession that judge certain journals important and others not. Using SSRN's main ranking, all of the top 25 free-market economists rank in the top 5 percent of all scholars listed on SSRN. Using other measures, the top six free-market economists also rank in the top 5 percent of all authors using the Eigenfactor Score™ and a composite score giving equal weights to all categories. Economists at the "third-rate MITs"[10] of the world appear to be producing a lot of work that few people care to read: the kelly green golf shoes. Surprisingly, scholars at these schools

Table 5

Top 25 American Economics Departments Ranked According to SSRN's Main Ranking Based on Total New Downloads

SSRN Main Ranking of Economics Departments	**University and Department**	Total New Downloads	**Total New Downloads Rank**	# of New Papers	**# of New Papers Rank**	New Downloads per Paper	**New Downloads Per Paper Rank**	All-Time Downloads	**All-Time Downloads Rank**	Citations	**Citations Rank**	# of Total Papers	**# of Papers Rank**	Downloads per Paper	**Downloads per Raper Rank**	Citations per Paper	**Citations per Paper Rank**	# of Authors	**# of Authors Rank**	Total Downlods per Author	**Total Downloads per Author Rank**	Total New Downloads per Author	**Total New Downloads per**	Citations per Author	**Citations per Author Rank**
1	**Harvard Economics**	37,870	**2**	264	**2**	13	**199**	409,042	**1**	89,122	**1**	2837	**1**	144	**99**	31	**1**	116	**6**	3,526	**4**	326	**14**	768	**1**
2	**Cornell Economics**	37,644	**3**	41	**66**	126	**2**	79,851	**20**	2,512	**51**	299	**71**	267	**19**	8	**72**	45	**62**	1,774	**27**	837	**1**	56	**90**
3	**MIT Economics**	32,122	**6**	203	**3**	19	**112**	285,668	**3**	38,353	**2**	1691	**3**	169	**63**	23	**4**	79	**17**	3,616	**3**	407	**9**	485	**2**
4	**NYU Stern Economics**	22,444	**8**	92	**20**	19	**112**	154,758	**6**	21,936	**4**	1194	**6**	130	**126**	18	**11**	51	**52**	3,034	**6**	440	**6**	430	**4**
5	**Princeton Economics**	18,256	**9**	90	**22**	21	**93**	122,180	**11**	17,864	**5**	885	**9**	138	**112**	20	**7**	76	**19**	1,608	**32**	240	**34**	235	**10**
6	**UC Berkeley Economics**	16,731	**10**	134	**5**	13	**199**	129,700	**9**	26,267	**3**	1306	**4**	99	**199**	20	**7**	91	**10**	1,425	**42**	184	**54**	289	**8**
7	**Brown Economics**	16,219	**12**	56	**39**	30	**39**	154,726	**7**	14,656	**6**	541	**27**	286	**17**	27	**2**	65	**31**	2,380	**15**	250	**30**	225	**11**
8	**George Mason Economics**	15,261	**13**	125	**7**	30	**39**	48,572	**37**	742	**133**	514	**30**	94	**224**	1	**387**	58	**39**	837	**116**	263	**26**	13	**253**
9	**Duke Economics**	14,615	**14**	94	**16**	19	**112**	115,031	**12**	9,721	**14**	763	**13**	151	**87**	13	**26**	82	**15**	1,403	**47**	178	**58**	119	**27**
10	**Stanford Economics**	12,953	**16**	76	**27**	21	**93**	128,379	**10**	7,890	**18**	621	**21**	207	**38**	13	**26**	58	**39**	2,213	**20**	223	**39**	136	**23**
11	**U Pennsylvania Econonomics**	12,581	**17**	123	**8**	14	**188**	114,643	**13**	11,483	**10**	921	**8**	124	**147**	12	**30**	75	**20**	1,529	**35**	168	**65**	153	**19**
12	**USC Marshall Finance & Business Econ**	10,914	**20**	21	**136**	54	**11**	67,247	**25**	2,417	**54**	203	**109**	331	**9**	12	**30**	26	**145**	2,586	**10**	420	**7**	93	**48**
13	**USC Economics**	9,949	**21**	29	**88**	37	**22**	98,658	**15**	4,858	**27**	271	**76**	364	**6**	18	**11**	34	**94**	2,902	**8**	293	**22**	143	**21**
14	**University of Chicago Econ**	8,529	**28**	92	**20**	11	**258**	79,322	**21**	13,784	**7**	770	**12**	103	**188**	18	**11**	70	**26**	1,133	**65**	122	**99**	197	**13**
15	**Dartmouth Econ**	8,317	**29**	93	**19**	11	**258**	72,874	**22**	11,075	**11**	774	**11**	94	**224**	14	**20**	30	**118**	2,429	**13**	277	**23**	369	**6**
16	**Claremont,R. Day School of Econ & Finance**	8,231	**31**	31	**81**	28	**50**	70,055	**24**	1,692	**74**	292	**72**	240	**26**	6	**106**	30	**118**	2,335	**17**	274	**25**	56	**90**
17	**Bard College—Levy Economics Institute**	8,219	**32**	69	**30**	18	**124**	55,303	**30**	853	**123**	447	**37**	124	**147**	2	**285**	86	**11**	643	**176**	96	**143**	10	**284**
18	**Yale Economics**	7,691	**33**	60	**37**	15	**161**	55,616	**29**	4,236	**33**	507	**31**	110	**174**	8	**72**	58	**39**	959	**89**	133	**88**	73	**60**
19	**University of Maryland Economics**	7,226	**36**	69	**30**	11	**258**	71,613	**23**	8,374	**16**	679	**17**	105	**186**	12	**30**	74	**21**	968	**87**	98	**137**	113	**30**
20	**Cornell Applied Econ & Management**	6,999	**37**	52	**48**	19	**112**	54,647	**31**	2,506	**52**	359	**55**	152	**86**	7	**84**	39	**74**	1,401	**48**	179	**57**	64	**73**
21	**Boston College Economics**	6,983	**38**	33	**78**	27	**55**	39,697	**48**	3,419	**39**	257	**87**	154	**83**	13	**26**	28	**128**	1,418	**44**	249	**31**	122	**25**
22	**Rutgers Newark, School of Bus, Finance & Econ**	6,474	**39**	23	**120**	45	**16**	37,987	**51**	2,057	**64**	144	**150**	264	**21**	14	**20**	22	**183**	1,727	**29**	294	**21**	94	**47**
23	**Michigan at Ann Arbor Economics**	6,043	**42**	78	**24**	9	**320**	44,168	**42**	9,870	**13**	679	**17**	65	**368**	15	**18**	73	**23**	605	**194**	83	**175**	135	**24**
24	**Columbia, Arts and Sciences, Economics**	5,624	**45**	55	**41**	7	**387**	60,091	**28**	12,926	**8**	754	**14**	80	**290**	17	**16**	70	**26**	858	**108**	80	**186**	185	**14**
25	**UC Santa Cruz Economics**	5,422	**49**	51	**51**	9	**320**	51,716	**34**	3,762	**35**	621	**21**	83	**267**	6	**106**	35	**90**	1,478	**38**	155	**70**	107	**38**

are often quite arrogant about their achievements or lack thereof. But if few people are reading these mainstream economists' work now, will they have much lasting influence in the future? In contrast, the top free-market economists are producing work that people actually care about. Rather than writing simply to show academic prowess or establish an academic pecking order, many free-market economists write because they consider economic ideas powerful and they are passionate about the implications of their work (Sutter 2007: 57). In their theories of social change, free-market economists including Mises, Hayek, and Rothbard believed in the importance of winning the battle of economic ideas (Caplan and Stringham 2005; Stringham and Hummel 2010). That free-market economists are among the best-read economists is likely a positive sign of future influence.

Notes

1. Imagine if the *New York Times* Best Seller List did not look at book sales, but simply looked at whether an editor accepted a book for publication. The measure of popularity would not be among actual readers but among a select few.

2. An author can write a book that is widely cited in SSCI journals, but those citations are not counted. An author can write an article that is widely cited in SSCI journals, but if the article is not in an SSCI journal, then those citations are not counted. An author can write an article in an SSCI journal that is widely cited in books or non-SSCI journals, and those citations are not counted.

3. Lee et al. (2010: 1040) write: "Mainstream and heterodox economics are distinct alternative subdisciplines within economics, based on having distinct bodies of theoretical knowledge and problems and puzzles to investigate. Moreover, being distinct bodies of knowledge, it is quite possible that the processes of building scientific knowledge are different enough so to generate distinctly different referencing and citation practices."

4. SSRN classifies new as occurring within the past year.

5. SSRN reports: "Eigenfactor™ is a weighted measure of an author's citations. It adjusts for the number of authors of the paper, the number of outgoing citations from each paper citing an author's paper and for the importance of the citing paper as measured by its Eigenfactor Score. All self citations are eliminated in calculating an author's Eigenfactor Score. The Score reported in the SSRN ranking tables is calculated from SSRN citation data only. To understand how this importance-weighting works, consider the following iterated voting procedure. 'Each author begins with a single vote and passes

it on, dividing the vote equally among those authors whom she cites. After one round of this procedure, some authors will receive more votes than others. In the second round, each author passes on her current vote total, as received in the previous round, again dividing this quantity equally among those authors whom she cites. This process is iterated indefinitely. Eventually, we reach a steady state in which each author receives an unchanging number of votes in each round. (We require irreducibility and aperiodicity.) An author's Eigenfactor Score is the percentage of the total votes that she receives at this steady state.' For further explanation and examples of Eigenfactor Scores see: http://www.eigenfactor.org/methods.htm."

6. The average age of the 10 free-market economists who are unlisted in SSRN is well over 65, so the sample of scholars on SSRN tends to be younger.

7. Some scholars have duplicate listings in the system, so these figures are not as precise as they appear.

8. The composite ranking equally weighted across all categories yields a top 10 of Leibowitz, Klein, Rubin, Smith, Hoover, Boettke, Margolis, Stringham, Krozner, and Graves in that order.

9. In the law school rankings George Mason University Law School, which is also home to many free-market scholars, ranks 18th, ahead of University of Virginia and Cornell.

10. Being a third-rate MIT is the common practice of economics departments attempting to mimic MIT while doing a much worse job.

References

Black, B., and P. L. Caron. (2006). "Ranking Law Schools: Using SSRN to Measure Scholarly Performance." *Indiana Law Journal* 81: 83–139.

Brown, L. D. (2003). "Ranking Journals Using Social Science Research Network Downloads." *Review of Quantitative Finance and Accounting* 20(3): 291–307.

Buchanan, J. M. (1964). "What Should Economists Do?" *Southern Economic Journal* 30(3): 213–222.

Caplan, B., and E. P. Stringham. (2005). "Mises, Bastiat, Public Opinion, and Public Choice." *Review of Political Economy* 17(1): 79–105.

Cohen, N. (2008). "Now Professors Get Their Star Rankings, Too." *New York Times*, June 9.

Copp, C. (1992). "Three Kinds of Economists: Memberships and Characteristics." *American Journal of Economics and Sociology* 51(1): 43–56

Economist, The (2011) "What Good Are Economics Journals?" *Economist: Free Exchange*, March 23. http://www.economist.com/blogs/freeexchange/2011/03/economics_3.

Hannon, K. (2010). "These Regular Folks Have Become 'Warren Buffetts Next Door'." *USA Today*, December 26.

Hirst, S. (2011). "Harvard Corporate Faculty Lead SSRN Rankings." The Harvard Law School Forum on Corporate Governance and Financial Regulation. The President and Fellows of Harvard College, January 11. Web. 25 Jun 2011. http://blogs.law.harvard.edu/corpgov/category/program-events/

Holcombe, R. G. (2004). "The National Research Council Ranking of Research Universities: Its Impact on Research in Economics." *EconJournalWatch* 1(3): 498–514.

Klein, D. B., and E. Chiang. (2004). "The Social Science Citation Index: A Black Box—With an Ideological Bias?" *EconJournalWatch* 1(1): 134–165.

Laband, D. N., and R. D. Tollison. (2000). "On Secondhandism and Scientific Appraisal." *Quarterly Journal of Austrian Economics* 3(1): 43–48.

Lee, F., B. C. Cronin, S. McConnell, and E. Dean. (2010). "Research Quality Rankings of Heterodox Economic Journals in a Contested Discipline." *American Journal of Economics and Sociology* 69(5): 1409–1452.

McCloskey, D. M. (1995). "Kelly Green Golf Shoes and the Intellectual Range from M to N." *Eastern Economic Journal* 21(3): 411–414.

Rosen, S. (1997). "Austrian and Neoclassical Economics: Any Gains from Trade?" *Journal of Economic Perspectives* 11 (4): 139–152.

Stringham, E. P., and J. R. Hummel. (2010). "If a Pure Market Economy Is So Good, Why Doesn't It Exist? The Importance of Changing Preferences Versus Incentives in Social Change." *Quarterly Journal of Austrian Economics* 13(2): 31–52.

Sutter, D. (2007). "Austrian Economics and the Market Test Reexamined." *Quarterly Journal of Austrian Economics* 10(1): 51–64.

——. (2012). "Measuring Scholarship in Free-Market Economics." Working paper, Troy University.

The Social Construction of Theoretical Landscapes: Some Economics of Economic Theories

By RICHARD E. WAGNER*

ABSTRACT. Economic theory emerges through interaction among interested participants, with the content of those theories being a product of spontaneous ordering and not scientific planning. At any moment, it is reasonable to expect various theoretical formulations to be in play, some typically receiving greater attention than others. As with spontaneous orders in general, the institutional arrangements within which theorizing occurs are influential though not determinative over the characteristics of theories. In this respect, a distinction is made between theories directed at understanding social processes as open and creative and theories directed at controlling what are treated as closed and deterministic processes. This distinction is illustrated with respect to theorizing about macro phenomena and public phenomena.

Economic theory is not generated through the aegis of some Minister of Economics. To the contrary, it is generated through open interaction among people who are interested in participating in that generation. It is a product of spontaneous ordering and not of planning. Each theorist, of course, plans his or her research activity, and theorists in turn might combine themselves into various organized groupings, and these groupings might differ in the influence they exert over the course of economic theory. Spontaneous ordering does not deny planning, but rather pertains to processes of unplanned interaction among plans. Thomas Schelling (1978) exemplifies spontaneous ordering as an emergent product of interaction among plans, and his framework surely pertains as well to the generation of economic theories as it pertains to the numerous phenomena he examines.

George Mason University, Department of Economics, 3G4, Fairfa, VA 22030, USA, rwagner@gmu.edu, http://mason.gmu.edu/~rwagner.

American Journal of Economics and Sociology, Vol. 71, No. 5 (November, 2012).

The analytical object denoted as an economy, moreover, cannot be observed. Particular factories or shops can be observed, but the variables of which economic theories are constituted mostly are not directly observable. Those variables are constructed with assistance from prior acts of theoretical articulation. One can observe particular marketplaces at specific locations; one cannot observe the abstract notion of a market economy. One can observe whether someone has a job; one cannot observe a rate of employment. Similarly, the distinction between endogenous and exogenous variables is not given by nature but is a product of theoretical construction. Just how the social construction of economic variables proceeds or might proceed under different institutional arrangements is the topic that animates this paper.

The practice of economics took place for millennia before theorizing about that practice began. While economic thought was present in classical Greece, as Todd Lowry (1987) examines, economics as an object of systematic study took root in medieval Spain, as Joseph Schumpeter (1954: 73–142) recognized and Marjorie Grice-Hutchinson (1978) explored. As late as the 18th century, economic theory was largely the province of amateurs. Only in the 19th century did economic theory become the province of professionals who earned their livelihoods by thinking about economics, as George Stigler (1965: 31–50) shows with respect to economics in Great Britain and the United States. This paper adopts a stylized comparison of amateurs and professionals to explore how different institutional arrangements might influence the character of theoretical formulations.[1] In this respect, Gordon Tullock (1967) explains that much science can be pursued by amateurs who do not require expensive equipment or facilities.

This article uses economic theory to explore the generation of economic theory. Where individual scholars are micro units in this analysis, the theoretical constructions that emerge are macro units. This micro-macro relationship points in two directions. From one direction, economic theory emerges through discussion and interaction among interested participants, which leads in turn to the emergence of professional associations and regular vehicles of communication. From the other direction, those paraphernalia operate to create and reinforce standards and rankings among contending formulations, thereby serving to push a discipline in particular directions. Assisting in this process is the attraction of outside interest in the activities of the associated set of scholars. In this way, the course of scholarship and the societal construction of theoretical formulations plausibly come to differ due to differences in the selection properties of different institutional arrangements.

This article turns on a comparison of two ideal typical frameworks within which economic theory might emerge. The first is where theorists self-finance their activities and the relationships among theorists are dyadic. The second is where theorists are financed significantly by third parties, with relationships among theorists becoming triadic. Following this comparison, the public significance of economic science is explored for possible implications regarding the generation of economic theories. The central distinction here is between economic theory as satisfying interests lodged in curiosity and as satisfying utilitarian interests. This distinction is explored for two substantive areas of economic theory: public economics and macroeconomics.

Theorizing as an Activity of Interested Amateurs

We can readily imagine a situation where a number of people find themselves wondering how it is that societies seem to exhibit generally orderly patterns of activity even though no person has the perception of having his or her activities directed by someone else. To use an image set forth in Wagner (2010), people do not perceive themselves as being members of a parade who are being directed by a parade marshal, and instead perceive themselves as one of the many persons passing through a busy piazza. Within this context, we recognize that some people start to think about how an account of societal orderliness might be given in the absence of some such directing entity as a parade marshal. One component of this effort would extend as well to the instances of disorder that can be recognized historically and is sometimes perceived through experience.

These inquiries would typically proceed through reading, writing, and discussion. Letters would circulate and one person's formulations would sometimes be used by other scholars in their own work, as illustrated, for instance, by interaction between David Hume and Adam Smith and between David Ricardo and Thomas Malthus, the latter of which is explored by Robert Dorfman (1989). A network would form consisting of such self-financed and independent scholars, who would make their ideas and findings available to other interested scholars. It would be normal to expect some of those formulations to attract more attention than other formulations. As self-financed scholars, it is reasonable to think that they were motivated largely by curiosity about how the world works and not by some utilitarian and external impetus to reshape the world. They were engaged in introversive and not extroversive labor, to recall Mises (1966: 587–588).

There is, however, no reason to think in this setting that there would be quick convergence on dominant explanations. A theory is a macro entity that is constituted through combining a number of smaller units of thought into some larger pattern. A theory can thus be broken into its constituent bits of thought, much like information can be broken into bits. In this setting, theorizing is an activity that takes place in combinatorial space. Suppose, for instance, that a typical act of theorization requires a selection of 10 bits from among 100 possible bits. In this instance there would be over 17 trillion possible theoretical formulations. Even on such a small explanatory scale, most of theoretical space would be unexplored. As some formulations gain attention from other interested parties, it is reasonable to expect that independence among those formulations will give way to a good deal of interdependence as some people give *a priori* credence to other formulations, as illustrated perhaps by information cascades (Bikhchandaini, Hirschleifer, and Welch 1992), the economizing features of which can serve to herd theorists and their theories in particular directions (Klein and Stern 2009).

Following the psychological claim about the magic number seven to indicate our limited mental faculties (Miller 1956), we might think that a relative handful of explanations will tend to be active at any instant due to the inability of people to handle more information than this, as Collins (1998) asserts in his treatment of scholarly competition combined with limited attention space. As scholarly activity comes to attract attention, however, the social setting of independent amateurs may not persist. Instead, new phenomena might emerge and these may exert independent effects on the course of scholarly inquiry. Much depends on whether scholarly relationships continue as largely dyadic in character or whether they become significantly triadic (Simmel 1900). When relationships are dyadic, scholars meet one another as equals, explore one another's formulations, and go forward from there. The posited framework of dyadic inquiry is an ideal type that is useful for organizing thought but is not a full description of reality.

Even in this setting, social configurations can arise to exert downward causation along the lines Paul Lewis explores (2012), and the internal operation of those configurations can influence the course of scientific inquiry. When those relationships become significantly triadic, networked interaction among amateurs gives way to interaction among professionals who are supported significantly by outside triads. The triad and its interests become significant participants in the generation of economic theory even though the triad might not engage directly in theoretical activity. The replacement of largely dyadic with significantly triadic relationships corresponds to a social transformation away from reflecting interaction among self-financed amateurs toward interaction among outside-financed professionals. Through the operation of downward causation, this alternative environmental arrangement modifies the operation of competitive selection among theoretical options, as an illustration of the ecological interaction between mind and environment that Gigerenzer (2008) explores in his treatment of ecological rationality as contrasted with as-if constructions of rationality.

The Emergence of Professional Paraphernalia

It is easy enough to imagine networks of interested amateurs forming as scholars disseminate their work to interested parties. Even where amateurs self-finance their scholarly activities, various professional paraphernalia are likely to emerge. The source of that emergence would reside in the ability of those paraphernalia to advance the scholarly interests of the participants. This would describe a world of uni-directional causation, where interactions among people create social configurations that facilitate those interactions. Among those paraphernalia would be scholarly journals and magazines and professional associations and meetings. In this uni-directional setting, scholarly networks would be scalable. Networks would differ in size, but connections within those networks would be random regardless of scale. This process could easily be characterized as a bottom-up process where interactions among interested scholars lead to the emergence of those higher-level phenomena. Those phenomena, however, can also serve to channel scholarly activity in particular directions, in which case causation runs downward as well as upward. In the upward direction, interaction among scholars generates the emergent phenomena we identify as professional associations and conventions. In the downward direction, those associations and conventions channel scholarly effort differently from what it is likely to have been before the emergence of those associations and conventions.

Many networks are scale-free and not random, as Barabási (2002) explains. If so, some nodes within a network take on particular significance as hubs as scale expands, generating highly skewed distributions of influence. Such skewness perhaps illustrates a form of downward causation where macro-level formations influence micro-level action. The emergence of journals and professional associations creates a communication path that runs in two directions: one direction runs from individual scholars and their activities to the emergent scholarly paraphernalia; the other direction runs from that scholarly paraphernalia to the individual scholars, influencing the direction of their scholarly activities. The upward direction is easy enough to understand, and fits well with the basic outline of economic theory, which runs from such human actions as choices among products to such emergent phenomena as market prices. The downward direction, which has less presence in economic theory, is one where higher-level social configurations influence the framing of options for choice at the lower level. This is the direction by which the emergence of professional journals and associations can influence the kinds of topics that scholars explore.

What sets the stage for this movement from top to bottom is the limited attention space that scholars have (Collins 1998). With respect to theorizing in combinatorial space, we can think of theories that cluster in the same neighborhood while other theories are located in different parts of the theoretical space. Those that cluster in the same neighborhood could be regarded as belonging to the same school or style of thought. While much scholarly work takes the form of plumbing the depths of some particular scholarly insight in that particular part of combinatorial space, it is also a normal as well as a prudent facet of scholarly activity to keep some track of neighboring scholarly programs. After all, all scholarship involves peering into unknown territory and it is always wise to pay some attention to other explorers.

Such emergent phenomena would inhabit the world of self-financed amateurs whose relationships with one another are dyadic and mutual even if not expressly contractual. During the 19th century, scholarship by amateurs increasingly gave way to scholarship by professionals. In this respect, Stigler (1965: 39–44) notes that publication in literary journals gave way to publication in professional journals during the 19th century. Whereas scholarship is financed by participants in a world of amateurs, it is financed to a significant extent by outside sources in a world of professionals. The dyadic relationships that are central to a world of amateurs give way to the triadic relationships that are the hallmark of the contemporary world of professional scholarship.

In a triadic world, scholars must be responsive to outside sources of support as well as to one another. The demand for economics no longer comes only from other scholars but comes also from outside entities. Whether those triadic entities modify the pattern of scholarship or the way in which they modify it depends surely on the intensity of their interests and the relative significance of the support they offer. That outside support could well be dominated by curiosity. For instance, many people are doubtlessly interested in dark matter and black holes as reflections of curiosity about the cosmos, and such dyadic support could well engage the world of physics. Such curiosity could well lie behind much dyadic support for scholarly activity, as illustrated by the establishment of foundations as Holcombe (2000) examines. In this respect, there is a long history of scholarly activity being financed by private foundations created within the realm of civil society, largely through bequests left by people who had amassed wealth through industrial and commercial activity. But much scholarly activity is financed through governments, and this creates a situation that needs to be plumbed to some degree.

Economics as a Science of Public Significance

James Buchanan (1996) explains that economics is a science of public significance because its material is of natural interest to many people in society, as Boettke (2011) elaborates. The basic conceptual idea sensed by the Scholastics and later by the theorists of the Scottish Enlightenment entails an unraveling of a mystery: economic affairs display coherence and order even though there is no director who imposes that order. Ideas of spontaneous order seek to explain the self-ordering qualities that operate when human interaction is governed by an institutional framework centered on private property and freedom of contract. Spontaneous order allowed economists to compete with priests in bringing comfort to people's minds by illuminating mysteries (Nelson 1991; Viner 1972, 1978).

The ability of economic theories to attract public attention operates concomitantly to transform dyadic into triadic relationships. There are now people other than those who practice economic theory who are interested in economic ideas. That interest, however, can manifest itself in either of two polar forms: in one form the triads are spectators to the creations of theorists; in the other form the triads become participants. But how might that participation play out in the generation of economic theories? The public significance of economics speaks to form and not substance. It says that triadic interests will commingle with those of the theorists in the creation of economic theories. It does not, however, make any substantive claims about the content of those theories.

With respect to substance, the historical record presents a pattern that resembles two parallel trees, each of which has numerous branches. One tree is concerned with the explanation of states of affairs and resource allocations, with states denoted as equilibriums. David Ricardo and Léon Walras are both branches of this tree, though that tree also contains numerous other distinct branches. The state-oriented tree locates the analyst as standing apart from the analyzed object, thereby taking a god's-eye view of the object. The resulting theoretical formulations are closed in form, and are analyzed through exploring the comparative statics of different data.

The other tree is concerned with processes of development and the governance of human interaction. Carl Menger and Gustav Schmoller are two of the many branches of that tree. The process-oriented tree locates the analyst inside the analyzed object. The resulting theoretical formulations are open in form, and are analyzed through what might be described as emergent dynamics. It should be noted, however, that emergent dynamics has nothing in common with treating differential equations as expressing such dynamics, and rather reflects open-ended theories that are enshrouded in complexity and Shackellian unknowledge (Shackle 1972, 1974).

Explanations in terms of states of affairs and in terms of processes of development are both sensible points of intellectual orientation, but they are different and non-commensurable points as Wagner (2010) explains. In a world where economic theory is the province of amateurs, it is reasonable to expect both types of theoretical orientation to attract scholarly interest, as was indeed the case before the 19th century when economics became predominantly the province of professionals. While it is easy to imagine triadic sources of support that would share an interest in open-ended theories, in contemporary times those sources are largely governmental agencies, which in turn are surely arrayed predominantly in support of closed-form formulations.

Open-ended formulations do not lead easily or readily to the articulation of specific promises about political programs because the open-ended quality of systemic complexity and spontaneous ordering explains that all such promises can be advanced only in the presence of uncertainty and unknowledge. To the extent electoral competition operates through the articulation and selling of promises and visions associated with those promises, close-ended theoretical formulations are the suitable vehicle for refining those promises. Whatever might be the relative sizes of the state-oriented and process-oriented analytical trees when economic inquiry is predominantly the activity of amateurs, it is reasonable to expect the state-oriented tree to expand in relative size when inquiry is predominantly the activity of professionals who are supported largely through collective entities.

There is nothing necessarily sinister or distorting about this, as in many respects it reflects what might be described as a change in tastes along the lines that Daniel Sutter (2007) explores. To the extent the public significance of economic science attracts politically-expressed interest, as it almost surely will, we should expect to find the sort of Big Player influences that Roger Koppl (2002) identifies. In this regard, Wolfgang Drechsler (2011) notes that one significant problem with the predominant use of mathematics as a vehicle for presenting economic theory is that it reduces economic variables to quantities. It is not that reality tells us that those variables are quantities. It is that the prevailing theoretical constructions mostly transform them into quantities; static-oriented theory can readily accommodate hedonic reduction of quality to quantity via the presumption of equilibrium prices in conjunction with the presumption that people are properly characterized by utility functions and not lexicographic orderings. In contrast, Robert Pirsig (1974) makes a strong case for the significance of qualities. It may be possible hedonically to transform a Lamborghini into 10 Fords at prevailing prices. We may be equally sure, however, that no owner of a Lamborghini would accept 10 Fords in exchange. Distinct qualities are not reducible to some common quantity without imposing calculational presumptions that countenance that reduction.

Among other things, we should expect the love of curiosity to lose ground to the utilitarian calculations that operate within the precincts of State. All that is necessary is that people engaged in political practice find some economic formulations to offer assistance for their practice. The question that arises is how economic theory might be transformed into something of use to those triads who finance a good portion of economic scholarship. This transformation is rendered possible by the inherent public interest in the material of economic theory. For instance, it is surely a facet of human nature to be less than fully content with events in the external world. An economic theory grounded in ideas about complexity and spontaneous order might be capable of explaining the sources of discontent, but it will not typically offer much by way of remedy, other than, perhaps, to work harder, or better, or to counsel people to work through their various situations assisted by the various support offered within the precincts of civil society.

For a theory to offer remedies as against offering just explanation or understanding, it must treat its object as something that can be manipulated. As for how that manipulation might be carried out, the use of state power must be part of the answer because there is no option on the societal as distinct from the personal level. Hence, a competitive process of theory selection shifts the structure of scholarly competition in a direction that increases the extent to which theorists respond to the triadic demand for manipulation by crafting tools and language suitable for that task, and also by helping to create an ideological framework that supports that activity. There is nothing insidious about this process, as it is a natural manifestation of scholars responding to opportunities as they perceive them. Only now there are other participants in the creation of economic scholarship, participants whose interest resides more in the utility of control and in participating in the exercise of power and societal reformation than in the pursuit of curiosity. We should thus expect economic theory to address different questions and adopt modes of thought suitable for generating answers to those other questions. There will still be limits on the span of attention, but the clusters around which that attention centers will take on different configurations and locations in scholarly space, to reflect the interests of the utilitarian users of economic scholarship.

Two Examples of the Economics of Generating Economic Theory

In this section I present two brief illustrations of the contrast between closed and open formulations of economic phenomena. In both cases, the intent is to illustrate that while open formulations may have realism and plausibility on their side, closed formulations have the ability to support rank orderings among political programs that open formulations might find difficult to articulate, and thus might be more attractive to people who seek actively to participate in political debate. First I will examine public economics or political economy as an example of competitive selection among theoretical formulations. Then I shall examine macro theory from the same orientation. Other fields could also be examined, but these two are the ones with which I am most familiar.

Public Economics and Political Economy

Modern states are too large and complex to be subject to hierarchical control, as Paul Craig Roberts (1971) explained for the Soviet Union and despite continual theoretical efforts to treat them in this fashion as exemplified by Drazen (2000) and Persson and Tabellini (2000). An economy is not a billiard ball that can be moved about by an expert-informed "Policy maker" striking the economy with a cue ball. An economy is rather a complex ecology of interacting enterprises, some organized on the market square and some organized on the public square, and with competitive and complementary relationships extending in many directions, as Wagner (2007) explains. In this vein, Roland McKean (1965, 1968) set forth a case for trying to elucidate an invisible hand in government to replace the vision of a planning state, and also Buchanan (1975).

Theories of political economy typically operate with a theoretical antinomy: market is taken to mean a complex network of enterprises where no one can even write out all of the detailed instructions necessary to make a pencil (Read 1958); in contrast, polity is taken to be a simple entity that is under direct control of some state agent. Theories of public finance and political economy typically work with a framework that entails an equilibrated economy that is acted upon by a political entity. Electoral competition is the process by which candidates compete for voter support to operate the levers of policy. That competitive process proceeds by offering diagnoses and remedies that are conveyed by a language that proceeds in definitive and deterministic terms. A claim that a particular tax measure will have a definitive and desirable impact on variables that people seem to care about creates a connection between an economic theorist and political candidates and their advisors. Claims that are accompanied by recognition of complexity and ambiguity in social phenomena may be of interest to people who seek to deepen their understanding of social phenomena but they do not provide much nourishment for the articulation of political programs.

The structure of mainstream economic theory with respect to collective activity seems adapted to service the reality that a large part of the demand for theoretical articulation arises from political offices that have programs to administer and politicians who are seeking language to support their articulation of programs. This process is supported by the image of State as a mechanic or as a manager of society, and this image fits comfortably with the framework of mainstream public finance. It's the image of public finance as concerned with applied statecraft and not with the explanation of social order as it pertains particularly to the role of collective activity in that order.

In contrast, public finance as concerned with social order would seek to explain from a departure in limited and distributed knowledge how collective activity meshes with, or fails to mesh with and perhaps even clashes with market activity. For instance, private athletic clubs provide equipment that generally matches the interests of their members. Among other things, clubs that provide facilities that are unused by their members will be failing to generate the income that could be generated from those premises. Clubs have good commercial reason to equip their facilities so as to reflect the preferences of their clientele. It is no different with a public park or playground. Only income is not generated through use, and yet the playground is equipped. Processes of economic calculation must be in play because there are always options, many of them. The park can be equipped in different ways, and the cost of equipping it one way is whatever value is foregone (and by whom?) by not equipping it differently. As Antonio De Viti de Marco (1936) noted, most theoretical work in public finance addresses questions of practical statecraft and not theoretical questions of political economy. De Viti, moreover, was not exclusively an academician. He was also a long-time member of the Italian Parliament as a member of the Liberal Party. He sought to sketch the contours of an explanatory theory, but this interest died in the 1930s, as Backhaus and Wagner (2005a, 2005b) explain.

We can ask: What makes for an interesting question for scholars to address? The answer will vary depending on the interests of the participants in the scholarly enterprise. When those participants are motivated largely by curiosity, patterns of scholarly inquiry will differ from what they will take on in the presence of utilitarian motivation combined with state-expressed interest in the results of scholarly inquiry. One source of demand for economic theories of collective activity is curiosity, and concerns efforts to explain and understand what we see going on around us. This motive for theorizing about economics is alive and well, but it accounts for but a part of the full demand for economic theorizing. There is also a demand that derives from utilitarian interests in sitting beside power. This interest need not be invidious. If economists do not sit beside power, other people will. Perhaps societal life will proceed better as more economists come to sit next to power than if those seats are taken by people from other occupations.

Macro Theory

Macro theory involves the relationship between the parts of something and the whole thing. With that thing being a society, micro theory would relate to individuals and macro theory would concern interaction among individuals. With societies, moreover, we are speaking of interaction among individual minds, which means in turn that acting on the macro object is not some such simple matter as striking the cue ball to move an object ball to a particular spot on the table. Macro economies are complex ecologies (Wagner 2012). They are constituted through interactions among micro entities that are simpler in nature than the macro ecology those entities generate.

With macro theory so conceived, the object is not subject to easy and ready manipulation or control. A macro theory of this style offers no handles for power to manipulate and control the ecology of plans. It also maps into an ideology that would counsel generally the avoidance of creating disorientation within the ecology rather than treating that ecology as a disordered garden to be spruced up through macro planning. The spontaneous order approach to macro phenomena would lead to a distinction between facilitating and directing. A policy that sought to facilitate the ability of participants within the ecology to pursue their plans might support the self-ordering processes at work within the ecology while a policy that sought to direct activity within the ecology would founder on the limited and distributed knowledge that characterizes all economic participants, both private and public.

In contrast, macro theories that speak directly of relationships between macro variables offer handles for the direct exercise of state power. If an economy is conceptualized as an ecology of plans, the extent of spending associated with one plan depends on perceived complementarities with other particular plans within the ecology. Macro-level performance emerges from the bottom and cannot be imposed from the top because the impact of any top-down imposition will depend on its ability to fit within and support the continually emerging ecology of plans, as De Grauwe (2010) suggests. In contrast, most macro models presume the existence of simple and direct relationships between macro variables. If people are observed to spend less privately, increased public spending might seem to be a way of boosting total spending, increasing employment in the process. Such formulations also have the property of appearing intuitively obvious, much as the observation that the sun rose in the east and set in the west appeared intuitively obvious before Copernicus.

While a good deal of economic theory has a self-generating character as economists revise and amend one another's formulations, much theoretical work also arises in response to external events. The experience of depressions is one such event that has undoubtedly induced much macro theorizing. We may be reasonably sure that the presence of triadic interests in macro phenomena will be strongly attracted to lines of explanation that provide a point for the insertion of control into the macro economy, which requires in turn an analytical framework where macro variables are direct objects of action. By contrast, open analytical frameworks do not readily support such control, or, alternatively, explain why efforts at control cannot claim theoretical support, recognition of which led Kochugovindan and Vriend (1998: 64) to summarize their paper thusly: ". . . because emergent phenomena are inherently unpredictable to some extent, the study of complex adaptive systems confirms that the true objective of science is not prediction but understanding." Once it is recognized that macro variables emerge out of micro-level interaction, there is no obvious place for the insertion of power to act directly on macro configurations because those configurations will also evolve in yet different directions as individuals respond to insertions of power.

Concluding Remarks on the Economics of Economic Theory

Economic theory, or any other field of scholarly inquiry for that matter, is not an object that anyone has designed. It is rather an object that has emerged through interaction among numerous interested participants. Significant features of that emergent object are surely open to explanation through economic theory, as Tollison (1986) and Eggertsson (1995) examine. To speak of emergence, moreover, is to think in terms of distinct levels of phenomena. On the lower level resides the scholars who are interested in thinking about their subject. Interaction among those scholars generates two types of higher-level phenomena. One type is the theoretical structure that emerges out of the efforts of the participating scholars. The other type is the various associations and journals that likewise emerge through that interaction.

Economics is a field with strong public interest, probably more so than many scientific fields. People interested in social insects seem likely to be dominated by curiosity types, as compared with economics. Whether a science is dominated by curiosity types or utilitarian types does not affect the competitive processes and interactions among scientists, for this competition is a feature of human nature. Humans create numerous cooperative relationships, and yet competition is present all the same. What results in any case is a species of spontaneous ordering among hobbyists who self-finance their activities.

The public character of economic theory generates a new source of demand for economic scholarship, and at the same time it transforms that generation into a new institutional environment. An environment dominated by amateurs is one of self-financing and private property. Within this environment particular patterns of scholarly inquiry would reflect Gigerenzer's (2008) notion of ecological rationality. With growth in triadic support in light of the public interest in economic articulation, there is a change in the environment within which economists generate economic theories. Economic theorists are rational creatures who always practice their craft within some particular environment. While there is always a logic of practice (Bourdieu 1990), the environment within which the craft is practiced will likewise influence the qualities of that craftsmanship.

There are two further facets to the collective expression of demand. One speaks to particular fields of activity. This is the content of theories that have been formulated to address if not to answer questions that have appeared on some public agenda. This activity requires theoretical formulations that render the public agenda sensible. A theoretical formulation that seeks to derive estimates of optimal tax progressivity supports a treatment of taxes and not prices as the proper means of financing government. A theoretical formulation that explains how state spending might affect aggregate income and employment is a formulation that feeds into a presumption that government can and should exert such influence.

Hence, theories also play significant ideological roles that perhaps were not part of the intention of the theorists who contributed to the construction of those theories. By operating with a framework where so-called macro policy acts on society as an entity, the theory supports an ideology that the state is a non-discriminatory entity that is pursuing a program of securing the public interest in difficult times. In contrast, a theory that treats the macro economy as a complex ecology of plans would dissolve the image of polity acting on society in general and in non-discriminatory fashion and would replace it with an image of polity acting within society by favoring some enterprises and activities over others. This form of alternative ideology might in turn serve to undermine some of the utilitarian demand for economic scholarship, influencing the future course of economic scholarship in the process. In any case, economic principles are surely as much in play in the generation of economic scholarship as they are in play in the generation and organization of other types of scholarly activity, as examined with respect to the organization of scientific inquiry by Kealey (1996), with respect to inquiry within economics by Reder (1999), and with respect to the generation of status rankings within universities by Burris (2004).

Note

1. It should be noted that the distinction between amateurs and professionals is not a judgment about quality. It is a distinction based on motivation. Amateurs do what they do out of curiosity and love for their chosen topic. Professionals do it because they are paid to do it. Without doubt, there are

professionals who do what they do out of curiosity and love for their chosen subject, and so receive rents from pursuing their activities. Equally without doubt, there are professionals who operate on various margins of indifference between scholarly and related activities and who choose based on relative returns.

References

Backhaus, J. G., and R. E. Wagner. (2005a). "From Continental Public Finance to Public Choice: Mapping Continuity." *History of Political Economy*, Annual Supplement 37: 314–332.

——. (2005b). "Continental Public Finance: Mapping and Recovering a Tradition." *Journal of Public Finance and Public Choice* 23: 43–67.

Barabási, A-L. (2002). *Linked: The New Science of Networks*, Cambridge, MA: Perseus.

Bikhchandaini, S., D. Hirschleifer, and I. Welch. (1992). "A Theory of Fads, Fashion, Custom, and Cultural Change as Information Cascades." *Journal of Political Economy* 100: 992–1026.

Boettke, P. J. (2011). "Teaching Economics, Appreciating Spontaneous Order, and Economics as a Public Science." *Journal of Economic Behavior and Organization* 80: 265–274.

Bourdieu, P. (1990). *The Logic of Practice.* Stanford, CA: Stanford University Press.

Buchanan, J. M. (1975). "Public Finance and Public Choice." *National Tax Journal* 28: 383–394.

——. (1996). "Economics as a Public Science." Pp. 30–36 in *How Do Economists Do Economics?* Eds. S. G. Medema and W. J. Samuels. Cheltenham, UK: Edward Elgar.

Burris, V. (2004). "The Academic Caste System: Prestige Hierarchies in Ph.D. Exchange Networks." *American Sociological Review* 69: 239–64.

Collins, R. (1998). *The Sociology of Philosophies: A Global Theory of Intellectual Change.* Cambridge: Harvard University Press.

De Grauwe, P. (2010). "Top-Down Versus Bottom-Up Macroeconomics." *CESifo Economic Studies* 56: 465–497.

De Viti de Marco, A. (1936). *First Principles of Public Finance.* London: Jonathan Cape.

Dorfman, R. (1989). "Thomas Robert Malthus and David Ricardo." *Journal of Economic Perspectives* 3: 153–164.

Drazen, A. (2000). *Political Economy in Macroeconomics.* Princeton, NJ: Princeton University Press.

Drechsler, W. (2011). "Understanding the Problerms of Mathematical Economics." *Real-World Economics Review* 56: 45–57.

Eggertsson, T. (1995). "On the Economics of Economics." *Kyklos* 48: 201–210.

Gigerenzer, G. (2008). *Rationality for Mortals.* Oxford: Oxford University Press.

Grice-Hutchinson, M. (1978). *Early Economic Thought in Spain, 1177–1740.* London: Allen & Unwin.

Holcombe, R. G. (2000). *Writing Off Ideas: Taxation, Foundations, and Philanthropy in America.* Brunswick, NJ: Transaction Publishers.

Kealey, T. (1996). *The Economic Laws of Scientific Research.* New York: St. Martin's Press.

Klein, D. B., and C. Stern. (2009). "Groupthink in Academia: Majoritarian Departmental Politics and the Professional Pyramid." *Independent Review* 13: 585–600.

Kochugovindan, S., and N. J. Vriend. (1998). "Is the Study of Complex Adaptive Systems Going to Solve the Mystery of Adam Smith's 'Invisible Hand'?" *Independent Review* 3: 53–66.

Koppl, R. (2002). *Big Players and the Economic Theory of Expectations.* New York: Palgrave Macmillan.

Lewis, P. A. (2012). "Emergent Properties in the Work of Friedrich Hayek." *Journal of Economic Behavior and Organization* 82: 368–378.

Lowry, S. T. (1987). *The Archaeology of Economic Ideas: The Classical Greek Tradition.* Durham, NC: Duke University Press.

McKean, R. N. (1965). "The Unseen Hand in Government." *American Economic Review* 55: 496–505.

——. (1968). *Public Spending.* New York: McGraw-Hill.

Miller, G. A. (1956). "The Magic Number Seven, Plus or Minus Two." *Psychological Review* 63: 81–97.

Mises, L. (1966). *Human Action,* 3rd ed. Chicago: Regnery.

Nelson, R. H. (1991). *Reaching for Heaven on Earth: The Theological Meaning of Economics.* Savage, MD: Roman & Littlefield.

Persson, T., and G. Tabellini. (2000). *Political Economics: Explaining Economic Policy.* Cambridge: MIT Press.

Pirsig, R. M. (1974). *Zen and the Art of Motorcycle Maintenance.* New York: William Morrow.

Read, L. (1958). *I, Pencil.* Irvington-on-Hudson, NY: Foundation for Economic Education.

Reder, M. W. (1999). *Economics: The Culture of a Controversial Science.* Chicago: University of Chicago Press.

Roberts, P. C. (1971). *Alienation and the Soviet Economy.* Albuquerque: University of New Mexico Press.

Schelling, T. C. (1978). *Micromotives and Macrobehavior.* New York: Norton.

Schumpeter, J. A. (1954). *History of Economic Analysis.* Oxford: Oxford University Press.

Shackle, G. L. S. (1972). *Epistemics & Economics.* Cambridge: Cambridge University Press.

——. (1974). *Keynesian Kaleidics.* Edinburgh: Edinburgh University Press.

Simmel, G. ([1900] 1978). *The Philosophy of Money.* London: Routledge.

Stigler, G. J. (1965). *Essays in the History of Economics.* Chicago: University of Chicago Press.

Sutter, D. (2007). "Austrian Economics and the Market Test Reconsidered." *Quarterly Journal of Austrian Economics* 10: 49–62.

Tollison, R. D. (1986). "Economists as the Subject of Economic Inquiry." *Southern Economic Journal* 52: 909–922.

Tullock, G. (1967). *The Organization of Inquiry.* Durham, NC: Duke University Press.

Viner, J. (1972). *The Role of Providence in the Social Order.* Princeton, NJ: Princeton University Press.

——. (1978). *Religious Thought and Economic Society: Four Chapters of an Unfinished Work.* Eds. J. Melitz and D. Winch. Durham, NC: Duke University Press.

Wagner, R. E. (2007). *Fiscal Sociology and the Theory of Public Finance.* Cheltenham, UK: Edward Elgar.

——. (2010). *Mind, Society, and Human Action: Time and Knowledge in a Theory of Social Economy.* London: Routledge.

——. (2012). "A Macro Economy as an Ecology of Plans." *Journal of Economic Behavior and Organization* 82: 433–444.

Economic Methodology and Nobel Laureates: Confirmation of a Methodological Paradigm Shift

By Brian Douglass*

ABSTRACT. Meir Kohn (2004) argues that two methodologies, the "value paradigm" and the "exchange paradigm," dominate modern economics with the equilibrium-focused value paradigm increasingly replaced by the more successful exchange paradigm. This article examines the question of modern economic methodologies and seeks to determine if the shift described by Kohn can be seen in the winners of the Nobel Prize in Economics (1969–2010). Trends in Nobel laureates suggest that Kohn's depiction of the two paradigms and their relationship appears accurate.

Meir Kohn and Methodological Divisions in Economics

Meir Kohn (2004) argues that two methodologies, the "value paradigm" and the "exchange paradigm," dominate modern economics. He suggests that the neo-classical, equilibrium-focused value paradigm is being replaced by the more successful exchange paradigm. This paper examines the question of modern economic methodologies and seeks to determine if the shift described by Kohn can be seen in the winners of the Nobel Prize in Economics (1969–2010). An analysis of the data shows that indeed this pattern described by Kohn can be seen in Nobel laureates.

Kohn (2007: 201) states that the value paradigm tries to describe the entire economy in terms of "value-theoretic equilibrium." Kohn describes the exchange paradigm as a variety of schools of thought that reject the value paradigm's view and instead describe the

*Brian Douglass lives in St. Louis, MO where he is a project coordinator for a non-profit engaged in neighborhood revitalization, Rebuilding Together-St. Louis. Email: bdouglass@gmail.com

American Journal of Economics and Sociology, Vol. 71, No. 5 (November, 2012).

economy "from the bottom up in terms of the problematic of individual transactions." He also notes that the exchange paradigm is "less mathematical and more institutional."

Similar patterns to Kohn's classification scheme have been recognized by others who have drawn similar conclusions on the nature of economic analysis. Williamson (1990) depicts economics as divided between "non-contractual," or "technological," and "contractual," or "institutional" approaches to analysis. Williamson states that the technological approach, similar to Kohn's value paradigm, dominated until 1960, while the contractual, Kohn's exchange paradigm, has gained increasing acceptance among economists in the last four decades of the 20th century. As Richard E. Wagner (2007) noted in his introduction to the special issue of *The Review of Austrian Economics* dedicated to Kohn's article, James Buchanan's 1964 paper "What Should Economists Do?" suggests the shortcomings of equilibrium analysis and that a distinction between the two camps can be seen as far back as Léon Walras and Carl Menger. Similarly, a history of the *American Economic Review* notes that: "Although in evidence well before World War II, the style of research in economics began to change, with emphasis on formal models, either graphical or mathematical *[value paradigm]* and, somewhat later, the routine use of econometrics in empirical analysis" *[exchange paradigm]* (Margo 2011: 20).

Kohn's division of economic methodologies seems to have strong support in the history of 20th-century economics and has been recognized, sometimes quite explicitly, by a number of economists. This article looks at the two methodological approaches offered by Kohn to see how they are represented in the winners of the Sveriges Riksbank Prize in Economic Sciences in Memory of Alfred Nobel. If Kohn and others are correct that what he terms the exchange paradigm is eclipsing the value paradigm, this change might be seen in the work of Nobel laureates.

Kohn's Methodological Paradigms and the Nobel Prize in Economics

Between 1969 and 2010, 66 individuals from around the world have become Nobel laureates for contributions to a number of economic fields. The published work of the winners of the Nobel Prizes was examined in order to chart the historical changes in economic methodology. Because award winners include economists who were active contributors to economics before the Great Depression and into the 21st century, this selection of prominent economists provides an interesting glimpse into the impact of changing methodology through the years on the field as a whole.

Because analysis of the entire corpus of all Nobel Prize winners since 1969 far exceeds the reasonable scope of this article, a decision was made to limit analysis to papers published in three of the top general economics journals: the *American Economic Review, The Journal of Political Economy*, and *The Quarterly Journal of Economics.* These three journals provide a sizeable sample of articles over the careers of the winners and contain many of their most notable contributions to the discipline. The rise of the value paradigm begins with the publication of Samuelson's 1947 *Foundations of Economic Analysis*; for the purpose of this study, the articles considered were limited to 1950 to 2010 for analysis, although papers prior to 1950 were tabulated for reference.

Using the search capabilities of the JSTOR database, the journal articles in question were tabulated by publication year, and the publication history of each winner before he or she was awarded the prize was examined. Because the prize is an award for the prior, lifetime work of each economist, only the work published before the award year was considered. Further, it is also likely that the increasing notoriety of laureates after an award would likely skew publication counts. In many cases, this proved to cover the majority of the laureate's career. Authors with fewer than four papers published in the three journals were not included in the trends analysis.

General Trends

With the publications tabulated by date for each of the award winners, a graph was produced showing each decade's award winners as a group and their publication years. This provided a visual confirmation of several trends in publication. As expected, those awarded prizes in earlier years tend to have more papers published in earlier years. The 2000s laureates' publication peak occurred between 1983 and 1985.

Figure 1

Laureates' Publications by Year

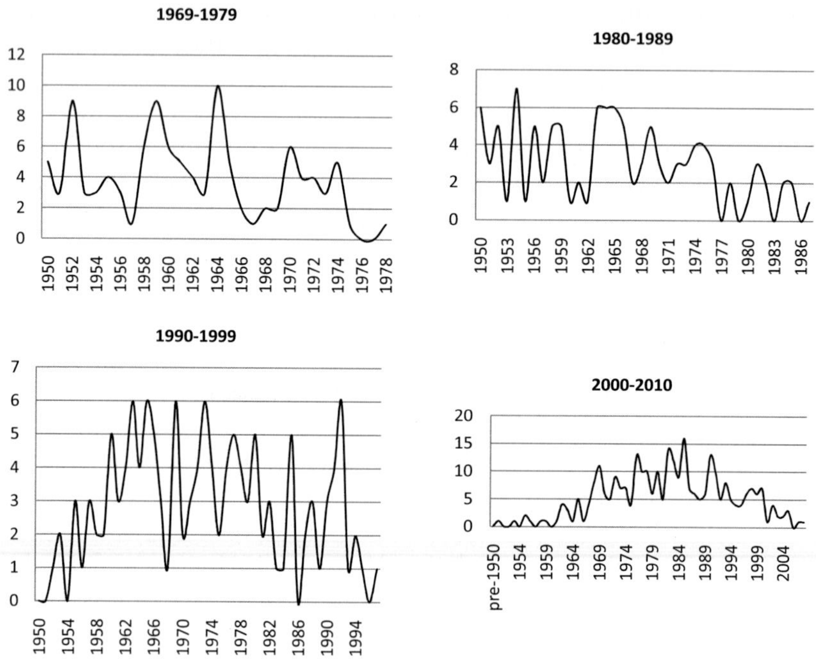

This pattern of publication peak of around 20–25 years prior to award is suggested by the 1980 and 1990 winners' publication data as shown in Figure 1. It is likely that this pattern becomes more pronounced in the later decades due to the fact that the full publication history can be taken into account in the more recent laureates.

Additionally, publication numbers tended to increase in the journals in question as time went on. This trend, however, was not necessarily indicative of any methodological change and may have more to do with the increasing prominence of research papers over other forms of content in economics journals, as well as the decline in the popularity of presenting research solely in book form, which was more the case prior to World War II (Margo 2011).

Methodologies and Nobel Prizes: Value Paradigm

When looking at the prevalence of the two methodological approaches identified by Kohn among Nobel laureates, one must first determine which individuals fit best into each paradigm. In "Value and Exchange," Kohn provides assistance in this area by proposing a list of key schools of thought as well as individuals who represent both the value and the exchange paradigms.

The value paradigm has two clear founders: Samuelson and Hicks, both of whom are laureates. Other individuals cited by Kohn (2004) as operating within this paradigm are Thomas Sargent, Robert Barro, and Nobel laureates Milton Friedman, Franco Modigliani, Robert Solow, Robert Lucas, and Paul Krugman.

The first decade of Nobel laureates in economics were, with two exceptions—F. A. Hayek and Herbert Simon—solidly in the value paradigm. The economists in this decade do raise some issues with data analysis considering the short window of time between the date of their award (1969–1978) and the publication of Paul Samuelson's *Foundations of Economic Analysis* (1947) compared to the winners of subsequent decades. Friedman also poses questions of classification due to his large corpus of publications and wide range of subjects. However, his 1970 article "A Theoretical Framework for Monetary Analysis," which lays out a mathematical formulation for monetary theory, has all the marks that Kohn notes as belonging to the value paradigm (Friedman 1970).

The 1969 inaugural award was presented to Ragnar Frisch and Jan Tinbergen "for having developed and applied dynamic models for the analysis of economic processes" (Nobel Foundation). The pair worked from a framework that had Walrasian roots, although Frisch is also remembered for his important work in econometrics, which has become a tool of choice for many in the exchange paradigm. John Hicks, along with Kenneth Arrow, received the award in 1972 for their contributions, which led to the creation of the value paradigm, in particular their work on equilibrium analysis and welfare theory. In the three journals examined, Samuelson's publications prior to his award remained in the double digits per decade in both the 1950s and 1960s and this pattern continued after his award; however, the peak occurred in the 1960s.

While Hicks did not publish any articles in the selected journals prior to the award of his Nobel prize, his fellow 1972 laureate Arrow did publish a number of papers, all of which show the mathematical rigor, particularly in the footnotes of several papers, that mark the value paradigm's efforts at economic modeling. The 1973 Nobel laureate, Wassily Leontief, also published most of his work prior to the period covered by this survey, but his work was in line with the program of the Samuelson-Hicks paradigm. In 1975, Tjalling C. Koopmans was awarded the prize. While his work dealt extensively with econometrics, he defended the value paradigm and its use of mathematical models of competitive equilibrium, placing him within the value paradigm methodology (Koopmans 1974).

The second decade of Nobel laureates in economics contains value paradigm representative Theodore Schultz (awarded 1979) who, among other subjects, applied value paradigm modeling to educational capital and the idea of an optimal level of such capital (Schultz 1960). James Tobin (awarded 1981) attempted to fix problems with previous value paradigm business cycle models as well as discussing financial and monetary models (Tobin 1955, 1968). Another economist who sought to address problems in the Sameulson-Hicks paradigm models was Solow (awarded 1987) who created his famous growth model, which bears the classical marks of value paradigm macroeconomics.

The 1985 and the 1990 awards were given to two other value paradigm economists: Modigliani and Merton Miller, who collaborated on a 1958 paper in the *American Economic Review* that developed a mathematical model attempting to describe how a firm makes financial decisions (Modigliani and Miller 1958). Not only was this listed as one of the most important papers to appear in the journal, but it also proved a foundational paper for modern financial economics (Arrow et al. 2011). This paper shows the key elements of a value paradigm model. It is large in scope, it is mathematical, and most tellingly, it views the firm as essentially a single, profit maximizing individual. Since Miller's award, the number of value paradigm laureates has markedly declined. Simultaneously, there has been an increase in winners from the fields of game theory and new institutional economics, which will be discussed below. Robert Lucas (awarded 1995) and Paul Krugman (awarded 2008) are the most recent value paradigm winners.

Methodologies and Nobel Prizes: Exchange Paradigm

Kohn provides a description of the exchange paradigm that provides no sharp divisions in terms of time. There is no equivalent of Samuelson for the exchange paradigm economists. The list of schools and fields that make use of this paradigm shows the broad spectrum encompassed by this research program. Kohn lists "new institutional economics, transactions cost economics, Austrian economics, public choice theory, law and economics and the economics of information" (Kohn 2004: 307).

When he names the important contributors to the exchange paradigm, Kohn lists "Coase, Alchian, Buchanan, Demsetz, Jensen, Kirzner, North, Olson, Williamson, Nelson, Romer, Akerlof, and Stiglitz" (Kohn 2004: 307). Of these, Buchanan, Coase, North, Akerlof, Stiglitz, and Williamson are Nobel winners. In contrast to the list of value paradigm laureates contained in Kohn's paper, this list is skewed towards the present day.

The list of Nobel laureates can be expanded further by examining the schools of thought associated with the exchange paradigm. To the list of fields given by Kohn could be added experimental economics as an area dominated by the exchange paradigm due to its tendency to look at empirical data (in this case, actual experiments rather than econometric analysis) and use those data to build theories from a micro level up. Another area, game theory, has produced a number of Nobel Prizes in recent decades. Game theory, as a whole, seems to fall outside either methodology; however, the economic applications of game theory have proven most useful when solving problems under the exchange paradigm framework.

The 2010 Nobel Prize in Economics was awarded to the developers of matching theory, which draws upon John Nash's work in game theory, as well as micro-level interactions, to develop a model that has been used to describe problems ranging from job matching to marriage. Without either game theory or the exchange paradigm, such work would not be possible. In the final analysis, such questions pose no significant change in the results, which vary little using different divisions of the methodological paradigm groupings, as can be seen in Figure 2.

While the bulk of exchange paradigm laureates are from the 1990s and 2000s, the notable exception to the modern-era awards trend is, of course, Hayek (awarded 1974). A similar case could be made for Simon (awarded 1978) due to his work on the internal decision-making process within a firm, which poses difficult questions for the assumptions of the value paradigm.

The 1980s saw Nobel Prizes awarded to George Stigler (awarded 1982) for his work on information economics as well as the previously mentioned James Buchanan (awarded 1986). In the 1990s, the number of exchange paradigm laureates came to dominate those who published in the journals under examination. In addition to Ronald Coase (awarded 1991) and Douglas North (awarded 1993), game theorists John Harsanyi, James Mirrlees, and William Vickery; new institutionalist economist Robert Fogel; and experimentalist Gary Becker were awarded prizes. In 1998, the prize was given to yet another economist who made use of exchange paradigm principles, Amartya Sen. Sen's use of social choice theory in order to consider human behavior in terms of social interaction and decision-making environments suggests a relation to Kohn's exchange paradigm (Sen 1970). He also applied this model to development economics, in particular, to the study of famine. In his paper "Ingredients of Famine Analysis" (1981) and book *Poverty and Famines: An Essay on Entitlement and Deprivation* (1983), Sen cites shortcomings in equilibrium models that do not take into account the impact local institutions, particularly social security and food distribution networks, which can allow mass starvation even in the presence of abundant food.

With the exception of Paul Krugman, every winner in the 21st century with more than three publications examined in this survey was a representative of the exchange paradigm. Peter Diamond, Dale Mortensen, and Christopher Pissarides won in 2010 for their work on matching theory, which has previously been discussed as an example of the use of the exchange paradigm in macroeconomics. Oliver

Figure 2

Publications by Paradigm

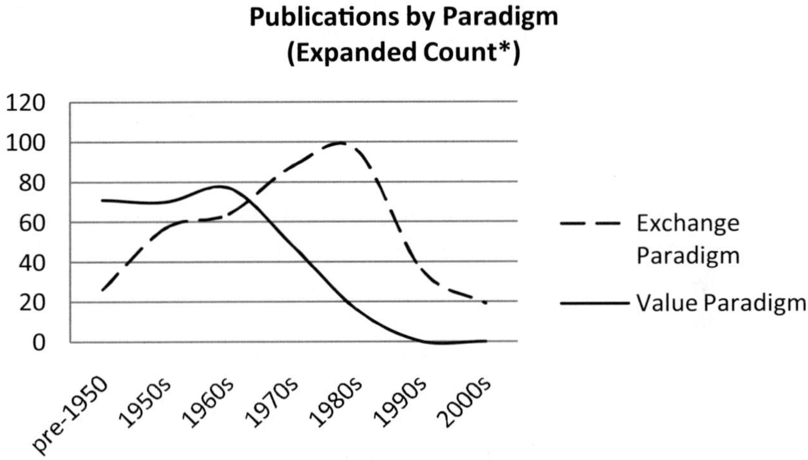

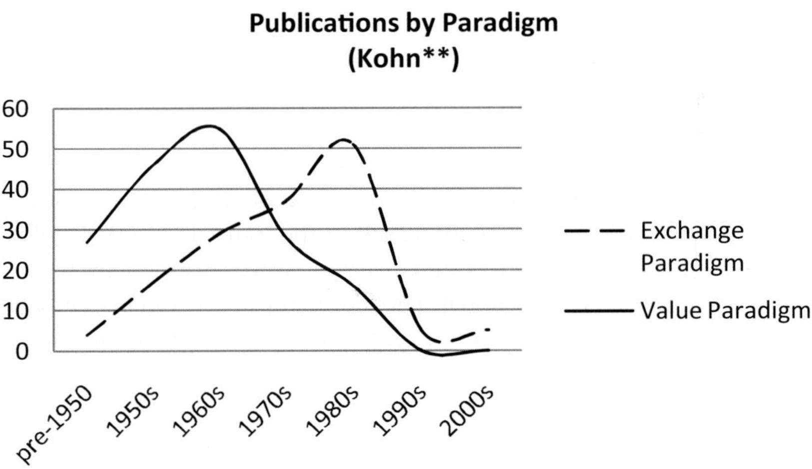

*Expanded count refers to the list that was obtained through my investigation of each Nobel laureate and subsequent classification of his work.
**This is based only on the names mentioned by Kohn in his article.

Williamson and Elinor Ostrom (awarded 2009) represent the new institutionalist school, which makes use of the exchange paradigm. Game theorists Leonid Hurwicz and Eric Maskin (awarded 2007) and Thomas Schelling (awarded 2005) and experimentalists Daniel Kahneman and Vernon Smith (awarded 2002) also received awards in the first decade of the 21st century.

In 2004, the award was given to Finn Kydland and Edward Prescott for their "contributions to dynamic macroeconomics: the time consistency of economic policy and the driving forces behind business cycles" (Nobel Foundation). This at first seems as if it is an area where value paradigm work would be expected. However, the pair's 1977 paper "Rules Rather than Discretion: The Inconsistency of Optimal Planning" implies a complexity and game-theoretic approach to individuals responding to government policies not just based on past statements, but how they expect the government to respond in the future (Kydland and Prescott 1977). This also implies that institutions matter. However, other work by Prescott and Kydland suggests a more value paradigm outlook on modeling (Kydland and Prescott 1982). Regardless, it is clear that by 1977 the two economists were certainly beginning to consider the impact of exchange-friendly elements on their models.

Table 1 lists the Nobel laureates considered in this survey of publications. Only those with publications in the selected journals during the time under study are included. This excludes, unfortunately, several laureates who did not publish in English-language journals as well as those who published primarily in the journals of other fields. Others, for example, Merton and Scholes, were awarded prizes for work on a specific question that does not really allow for classification into either paradigm, in their case derivative valuation (Nobel Foundation).

Analysis: Trends in Nobel Prizes and Methodology

One of the requirements established by the Nobel Prize committee is that awards be made only to living persons. This article has looked at Nobel winners as representatives of the top of the field of economics from the second half of the 20th century into the 21st. An

Table 1

Nobel Laureates by Paradigm

	Kohn (2004)	Author's (2012)	
Value	Friedman	Arrow	Tinbergen
	Hicks	Frisch	Tobin
	Krugman	Koopmans	
	Lucas	Leontief	
	Modigliani	Miller	
	Samuelson	Modigliani	
	Solow	Schultz	
Exchange	Akerlof	Becker	Nash
	Buchanan	Diamond	Ostrom
	Coase	Fogel	Pissarides
	North	Harsanyi	Prescott
	Stiglitz	Hayek	Schelling
	Williamson	Hurwicz	Sen
		Kahneman	Simon
		Kydland	Smith
		Maskin	Stigler
		Mirrlees	Vickery
		Mortensen	Williamson

examination of the top economics journal publications by the top economists of their era can reveal some general methodological trends.

Figure 2 shows that indeed a strong trend can be seen in the date of publication for each of the two paradigms. As the number of awards made to exchange paradigm economists leaves those of value paradigm economists behind in the 1980s, there is a similar trend in publication dates. The value paradigm reached a pre-award peak in the 1960s and declined while the exchange paradigm peaked in the 1980s. Due to the observed 20–25 year lag seen in Figure 1, this translates into a false decline for the exchange paradigm assuming that award trends remain the same. If the past is any indication, future awards to exchange paradigm economists will continue to move the peak through the 1980s and on towards the 1990s.

When the graphs of the expanded classification of economists is compared with the list of economists provided in Kohn, there is little significant change to the overall shape of the graphs in regards to time as shown above.

In order to simplify the analysis, the assumption was made that prizes were awarded near the end of an economist's working career and represented an award for his lifetime work as an economist. This is certainly not always the case as some laureates have written for many years after their award. However, such an assumption does provide a time at which to draw the line for each economist's publication history. Most economists have passed their publication peak output by the time they receive their Nobel Prize; furthermore, the prize is awarded for work done prior to the award, providing another reason for omitting later work. Given the approximately two-decade gap between observed peak of publication count and award year noted in Figure 1, this is yet another reason for looking at publications prior to the awarding of the prize.

Conclusion

Kohn's 2004 paper depicts the value paradigm as an older model, popularized by Sameulson in the 1950s, which he says is "reaching an impasse" and being replaced by the exchange paradigm. This seems to be confirmed by examining Nobel Prize winners as well as their publications.

By looking at the trend of Nobel laureates, it seems that the exchange paradigm is displacing the value paradigm when it comes to important advances in economics. Table 2 shows such a trend in both Kohn's as well as the author's classification of laureates. The data suggests a natural division occurring in the 1980s. A 60 percent (Kohn) and 71.6 percent (author's count) decline seen in Nobel laureates before and after this decade for the value paradigm indeed suggests stagnation if not replacement. Seeing not only a decline in publications and laureates, but also seeing the value paradigm laureates in increasingly rapid decline as we approach the 2010s, Kohn's depiction

Table 2

The Decline of the Prevalence of the Value Paradigm Laureates

		1960s	1970s	1980s	1990s	2000s		
Kohn	Exchange	0	0	1	2	3		
	Value	0	2	2	1	1	**pre-1980**	**post-1980**
	% Value Paradigm	N/A	100.0%	66.7%	50.0%	25.0%	100.0%	40.0%
Author's	Exchange	0	1	2	8	14		
	Value	1	7	2	2	1	**pre-1980**	**post-1980**
	% Value Paradigm	100.0%	87.5%	50.0%	20.0%	6.7%	88.9%	17.2%

of the two paradigms and his predictions for the future appear accurate and current trends suggest that his exchange paradigm is likely to maintain dominance in Nobel laureates for at least the next few decades.

References

Arrow, K. J., B. Bernheim, M. Feldstein, D. McFadden, J. Poterba, and R. Solow. (2011). "100 Years of the *American Economic Review*: The Top 20 Articles." *American Economic Review* 101(1): 1–8.

Friedman, M. (1970). "A Theoretical Framework for Monetary Analysis." *Journal of Political Economy* 78: 193–238.

Kohn, M. (2004). "Value and Exchange." *Cato Journal* 24(3): 303–339.

——. (2007). "The Exchange Paradigm: Where to Now?" *Review of Austrian Economics* 20: 201–203.

Koopmans, T. (1974). "Is the Theory of Competitive Equilibrium With It?" *American Economic Review* 64(2): 325–329.

Kydland, F., and E. Prescott (1977). "Rules Rather than Discretion: The Inconsistency of Optimal Plans."*Journal of Political Economy* 85(3): 473–492.

——. (1982). "Time to Build and Aggregate Fluctuations." *Econometrica* 50(6): 1345–1370.

Margo, R. (2011). "The Economic History of the *American Economic Review*: A Century's Explosion of Economics Research." *American Economic Review* 101(1): 9–35.

Modigliani, F., and M. Miller (1958). "The Cost of Capital, Corporation Finance, and the Theory of Investment." *American Economic Review* 48(3): 261–297.

Nobel Foundation."The Sveriges Riksbank Prize in Economic Sciences in Memory of Alfred Nobel." www.nobelprize.org/nobel_prizes/economics/.

Samuelson, Paul. (1947). *Foundations of Economic Analysis.* Cambridge: Harvard University Press.

Schultz, T. (1960). "Capital Formation by Education." *Journal of Political Economy* 68(6): 571–583.

Sen, A. (1970). "The Impossibility of a Paretian Liberal." *Journal of Political Economy* 78(1): 152–157.

——. (1981). "Ingredients of Famine Analysis: Availability and Entitlements." *Quarterly Journal of Economics* 96(3): 433–464.

——. (1983). *Poverty and Famines: An Essay on Entitlement and Deprivation.* New York: Oxford University Press.

Tobin, J. (1955). "A Dynamic Aggregative Model." *Journal of Political Economy* 63(2): 103–115.

——. (1968). "Notes on Optimal Monetary Growth." *Journal of Political Economy* 76(4): 833–859.

Wagner, R. (2007). "Value and Exchange: Two Windows for Economic Theorizing." *Review of Austrian Economics* 20: 97–103.

Williamson, O. (1990). "A Comparison of Alternative Approaches to Economic Methodology." *Journal of Institutional and Theoretical Economics* 146(1): 61–62.

The Impact of Nobel Prize Winners in Economics: Mainline vs. Mainstream*

By Peter J. Boettke†, Alexander Fink‡, and Daniel J. Smith§

Abstract. We assess the impact of two groups of economists: *mainline* economists, who regard economics primarily as the science of exchange and *mainstream* economists, who perceive economics primarily as the science of choice. To control for scholarly quality we investigate the citation impact of Nobel Prize winning economists, who we break up into the two groups, mainline and mainstream. We find that over the period from 1970 to 2007 mainline economists had more of an impact than mainstream economists.

> *Contemporary fame does not ensure lasting fame—the leaders of what prove to be scientific fads recede from even the histories of the science . . . This series of lectures is presented by economists [Nobel Laureates] who have met at least the requirement that their work has been recognized by contemporaries. A later age will separate the fundamental from the faddish contributions.*
>
> —George J. Stigler ([1985] 2009: 79)

> *But it is not the popular movement, but the traveling of the minds of men who sit in the seat of Adam Smith that is really serious and worthy of all attention.*
>
> —Lord Acton (1904: 212)

Introduction

Economics is a burgeoning field. The *Journal of Economic Literature* classification system has expanded from 10 general economic catego-

*We thank Thomas Hogan, Randy Holcombe, Daniel Klein, Peter Leeson, Douglas Rogers, David Skarbek, Daniel Sutter, the participants of the Documenting the Contribution of Dissident Scholars Panel at the Southern Economic Association 2011 Annual Conference, and an anonymous referee for comments on earlier versions of this paper. We gratefully acknowledge the financial support of the Mercatus Center at George Mason University. We also thank Danny Klöser for his valuable research assistance.

†Address: Department of Economics, George Mason University, Email: pboettke@GMU.edu.

‡Address: Institute for Economic Policy, University of Leipzig, Email: alexander.fink@uni-leipzig.de.

§Address: Manuel H. Johnson Center for Political Economy, Troy University, Email: djsmith@troy.edu.

American Journal of Economics and Sociology, Vol. 71, No. 5 (November, 2012).

ries and 45 subcategories in 1969, the year the first Nobel Prize in Economics was awarded, to 21 general economic categories and 132 subcategories in 2010. The average number of economic journals has expanded from 214 for the period from 1970 to 1979 to 824 journals for the years 2000 to 2007 (Kelly and Bruestle 2010). Despite the increase in quantity and diversity in scholarly output, we divide economists into two broad categories introduced by Boettke (2007, 2011)—*mainline* and *mainstream*—and analyze their respective impact on the discipline.

We understand mainline economists to work in the tradition of Adam Smith. They start with the postulate that shortsighted, cognitively limited individuals pursue their own self-interest.[1]

They focus their scholarly efforts on studying how these individuals, acting in their own self-interest, create complex social arrangements under the division of labor that align individual interest with the social interest. Thus, they tend to rely on invisible-hand theorizing to analyze how individuals coordinate individual plans in an orderly decentralized fashion (Ullmann-Margalit 1978; Nozick 1974: 18–22). Accordingly, mainline economists, tend to view economics primarily as the science of exchange, or *catallactics*. In slightly different words, based on the postulate of human purposefulness, they study exchange phenomena and the institutions within which exchanges take place in various social contexts. Following Adam Smith, mainline economists recognize the limits of economics as a tool for social control. Perhaps summed up best by Hayek (1988: 76), "[t]he curious task of economics is to demonstrate to men how little they really know about what they imagine they can design."

In contrast, we understand mainstream economists to tend to follow the scientific trends of their days and, at times, to be taken far afield from the mainline of economics by the pursuit of current fashions. For example, Boettke, Leeson, and Smith (2008) and Kreps (1997) argue that, in the 1930s, mainstream economists moved away from the advancement of the propositions explored by mainline economists. Instead of viewing economics primarily as the science of exchange, economics became a science of choice.[2] Rather than focusing their scholarly efforts towards studying the social arrangements that emerge to align individual and social interest, mainstream economists focused their attention on modeling the choice of cognitively perfect individuals in ideal situations, leaving no room for institutional analysis and operative mechanisms to explain how markets work given behavioral deviations from the hypothesized ideal man. In society, institutions emerge to cope with fallible men, and imperfect and incomplete information. Assuming these complexities away precludes the analysis of the institutions that emerge to overcome these barriers. The appreciation for complex and intricate social orders created through the invisible-hand of the market was gradually lost, opening the door to the use of economics as a tool of social control that dominated mainstream economic thinking in the 20th century.

This is not to say that mainstream and mainline economics are always diametrically opposed to each other. Influential intellectual entrepreneurs can swing avenues of fashionable inquiry found to be barren back to advancing the more fecund core propositions of the discipline. While analyses of exchange phenomena and the institutions that shape exchange took a back seat in the 1930s, the discipline was broadened again during the 1980s, as scholars like North (1994) and Ostrom (2010) brought the attention of the discipline back to advancing the mainline of economic inquiry.

We aim to assess the relative impact of mainline and mainstream economists on the advancement of economic inquiry. We do this by using the citation counts of the Nobel Prize Laureates—arguably the leaders of the economics profession—from 1969 to 2009.[3] We find that measured by annual citations, Nobel Laureates working in the mainline of economics have had a more enduring impact on the social science profession than those working in the mainstream of economics. Our conjecture is that while mainstream economists engage in fashionable scholarly pursuits, these pursuits over the long run tend to have a relative weak enduring influence on the economics profession. Alternatively, contributors to the mainline of economic thought focus their scholarly efforts on advancing core propositions of economics and have a relatively strong enduring impact on the profession.

We built two separate data sets. One, from 1970 to 2007, is based on the paper version of the Social Science Citation Index (SSCI),[4] which we refer to as the "non-electronic SSCI" database throughout the paper. The other dataset, from 1980 to 2007, is based on the electronic version of the SSCI provided by Thompson ISI, referred to as the "electronic SSCI" database throughout.

While our article is unique in its classification, the date range, and the nature of its data set, our article does build on previous work on the citation impact of Nobel Laureates. There has been previous work using citation counts of the Nobel Laureates to understand the characteristics of Nobel Prize winners, as well as their influence. Diamond (1988) gathered the citation counts for the 24 Nobel Laureates in economics from 1966–1980 and found that by working in the U.S., economists increased their chances of winning the Prize.[5] Skarbek (2009) examined the references of Nobel Laureates to other Nobel Laureates in the Prize Lectures given upon receipt of the Nobel. He found that Arrow, Hayek, Samuelson, Friedman, Lucas, and Phelps were the most cited by their Nobel peers in their Prize lectures.

There has also been work attempting to classify Nobel Laureates into different categories. Weinberg and Galenson (2005) classified the Nobel Laureates as either experimental, moderate conceptual, or extreme conceptual economists; experimental economists being those working inductively and conceptual economists being those working deductively. They found conceptual Noble Laureates to have made their most important contributions earlier in their careers, while experimental Laureates did so later in life.[6] Lindbeck (1985) split up Nobel Laureates into five categories, those who worked in general economic theory, made theoretical contributions concerning specific aspects or sectors of the economy, developed powerful new methods of economic analysis, conducted more "pure" empirical research, and those engaged in non-formalized innovative thinking. Lindbeck did not measure the citation impact of these groups.[7] Karier (2010) also broke down Nobel Laureates into several categories, including behaviorists, free market economists, number guys, and Keynesians, but did not measure the citation impact of the Laureates in these separate categories.[8] We contribute to this literature by offering a new categorization of economists—mainline vs. mainstream—and examining the citation impact of the Nobel Laureates belonging to these two groups.

The second section discusses differences in the perspectives of mainline and mainstream economists. The third section discusses the citation data. We present our results in the fourth section and conclude in the fifth.

Two Views of Economics: Mainline and Mainstream

The mainstream of the economics profession in the 20th century predominantly advanced economics as a science of choice (Williamson 2002: 172). Robbins (1932: 16) provided the according definition of economics that dominated the discipline, especially during the second part of the 20th century, by characterizing economics as "the science which studies human behaviour as a relationship between ends and scarce means which have alternative uses."[9] Accordingly, the majority of economists concentrated their effort on the advancement of theories of resource allocation instead of theories of market exchange and social cooperation under the division of labor (Buchanan 1964: 214). The focus on a narrow concept of choice as a solution to a given means-ends framework gave rise to the prevalent formulations of the theory of consumer behavior, the theory of the firm as a production function, and the theory of the benevolent social planner (Buchanan 2001; Williamson 2002: 172). Economic agents are assumed to "choose" to maximize, subject to constraints. Given that the means and ends are known to the chooser, the optimal choice is already implicit in the maximization problem under investigation. Economics then becomes a science devoted to solving given sets of problems and is more accurately regarded as a branch of applied mathematics (Buchanan 1964: 214). Market prices, which are an outcome of the market process, enter the problem as given parameters, and the coordination of plans, rather than being investigated as a process worthy of the attention of economists, is simply assumed by resort to a non-existent, and costless, auctioneer. These assumptions drain the prevailing equilibrium models of the very social elements that were at the core of Adam Smith's analysis, and assume away the very processes that economists should be attempting to understand (Buchanan 1964: 218).

While mathematical articulation of equilibrium, which the economy is constantly moving towards, was an important development in economics, exclusive focus on this static and never-realized end state pushes the examination of the very processes that tend the economy towards equilibrium to the periphery of scholarly attention. While, arguably, the initial formalizers of mathematical equilibrium understood it in the context of their training as invisible-hand theorizers, generations of scholars received their training and tenure by working exclusively in an institutionally sterile depiction of the world. This has produced a cadre of economic scholars who have failed to understand or appreciate the market as a process or the world in all of its complexity (Boettke 2012: 266). Mathematical formulations of the economy, unless a scholar is careful to contextualize his or her results, tend to assume away the complexity of the world, rather than focusing attention on the rich historical and institutional details of the world that warranted the most scholarly attention from Adam Smith. For example, while the first and second welfare theorem are held to prove that Adam Smith's theories were right, the strict conditions necessary for these mathematical articulations to hold necessitate corrective government action for those scholars who fail to appreciate the invisible-hand processes operative in the exchanges taking place in society.

It is important to note that the distinguishing factor between mainline and mainstream economists does not hinge on the use of mathematics. In fact, many of the economists we classify as contributors to the mainline of economic thought regularly employ mathematics. Rather, mathematics is a useful tool for economists, but can lead to an under appreciation of the invisible-hand processes of the world when the particularly human subject matter of economics is allowed to be marginalized or lost. In addition, the exclusive focus on mathematical representations of the economy may attract and encourage an engineering attitude among economists; precisely the "man of the system" attitude that Adam Smith warned about.

Alternatively, understanding economics as a science of mutually beneficial exchange opens the door for "invisible-hand explanations" of social phenomena (Nozick 1974: 18–22). Mainline economists consider economics primarily as a *social* science devoted to the analysis of the mutually advantageous interactions among individuals in the market. For mainline economists, "trade" and "agreement" (Buchanan 1964: 218) or "contract" (Williamson 2002: 172) take center stage, not socially isolated utility maximization. This is not to say that there is no place for what Hayek (1937: 46) coined "the pure logic of choice" in mainline theorizing. Some human behavior is devoted to the self-interested allocation of scarce resources among alternative ends. However, mainline economists eschew the sole reliance on this thin model of human behavior, but regard humans as capable, but "complex, fallible learners" (Ostrom 1997: 9). For mainline economists the theory of choice is at the Lakatosian "hard core" of economic theory,[10] but they consider uniquely economic problems to arise when exchanges enter the picture—when Friday arrives on the island—and institutions become necessary to structure human interaction.

Economists who perceive economics primarily as the science of exchange therefore concern themselves with understanding the impact of alternative institutional arrangements on human behavior and with the evolution of institutions. Their investigations comprise the evolution of legal, political, and other social institutions as they make up the set of relationships that is referred to as "the market" as well as organizations that populate the marketplace and the political sphere. In Coase's (1978: 206–207) words, "what economists study is the working of the social institutions which bind together the economic system: firms, markets for goods and services, labour markets, capital markets, the banking system, international trade, and so on." Thereby the sources of change are not limited to exogenous factors, as change can also emerge from within the institutional structures. Buchanan (1964: 218) provides an example of the explicit consideration of institutions as contingent to social interaction,

> A market becomes competitive, and competitive rules come to be established as institutions emerge to place limits on individual behavior patterns. It is this becoming process, brought about by the continuous pressure of human behavior in exchange, that is the central part of our discipline, if we have one, not the dry-rot of postulated perfection.

North (1994: 213) points out that the mainstream approach misses the significant role of different institutional regimes that characterized the rise of the developed western world. In contrast, besides trying to understand the formation of institutions better, mainline economists

Table 1

Classification of Mainline and Mainstream Nobel Laureates

Mainline	Mainstream			
Becker	Akerlof	Kahneman	Mirrlees	Simon
Buchanan	Allais	Kantorovich	Modigliani	Solow
Coase	Arrow	Klein	Mundell	Spence
Friedman	Aumann	Koopmans	Myerson	Stiglitz
Hayek	Debreu	Krugman	Myrdal	Stone
Kydland	Engle	Kuznets	Nash	Tinbergen
Lucas	Fogel	Leontief	Ohlin	Tobin
North	Frisch	Lewis	Phelps	Vickrey
Ostrom	Granger	Markowitz	Samuelson	
Prescott	Haavelmo	Maskin	Scholes	
Schelling	Harsanyi	Meade	Schultz	
Smith	Heckman	McFadden	Selten	
Stigler	Hicks	Merton	Sen	
Williamson	Hurwicz	Miller	Sharpe	

devote efforts to a better understanding of the functioning of alternative institutional regimes.

We expect the impact of the work of mainline economists to depend less on its conformity with contemporary conventions than the impact of the work by mainstream economists. We therefore expect mainline economists who work on the advancement of the core propositions of the discipline to have a more significant long-run impact on the social science profession than mainstream economists. To measure this, we use citation data of the Nobel Laureates in economics to measure the relative impact of these scholars on the profession. We split Nobel Laureates into mainline and mainstream categories based upon their adherence to the above outlined distinctions in Table 1.

Citation Data

We measure a scholar's success by the number of annual Social Science Citation Index citation counts. We focus on Nobel Laureates because at some point in time their work is considered to be of high scientific value independent of their mainline or mainstream orientation. Comparing Nobel Prize winners who belong in either one of the two groups allows us to control for scholarly quality.

We use the number of annual citations a scholar receives as a proxy for his impact on the social science profession. Vernon Smith (1974: 320) asserts that if a scholarly direction "leads to something insightful, it will command a respectable following." And followers generate references. The number of references to an economist's work is therefore one available measure of a scholar's impact. According to Landes and Posner (1976: 251) citations are an appropriate measure of a scholar's impact because "the normal function of the scholarly citation is . . . to give credit for prior original work, to refer the reader to corroborative or collateral findings by other scholars, and as a method of incorporating by reference, relevant theorems, proofs, etc."[11]

The SSCI has been published annually since 1966 (Diamond 1988). We collected the data at the Library of Congress, where annual citation counts are available from 1970 onwards for the non-electronic SSCI. The electronic SSCI only includes articles published after 1980. We collected citation count data from both databases up to the year 2007.

Both the non-electronic and the electronic SSCI databases suffer from several shortcomings. First, the SSCI does not distinguish between authors who share the same name. Therefore, it is difficult to determine the citation impact of an author who has a popular last name. This is especially true when the citing author does not include any middle initials (Klein and Chiang 2004: 137). Second, the SSCI database includes self-citations, skewing the record in favor of those who are the most self-promoting (Klein and Chiang 2004: 138). Third, the electronic Thompson ISI SSCI database gives a citation count to each author of a published work. Co-authored work counts as much as an individually crafted work (Klein and Chiang 2004). In contrast, the non-electronic database only reports the first listed author from an article, and not any co-authors (Alexander and Mabry 1994; Chung, Cox, and Okunade 1993; Diamond 1988; Medoff 1989). Cole and Cole (1973) argue that, empirically, this does not appear to have a substantial effect on the rankings. Since the vast majority of Noble Prize winners' major works are solo endeavors (van Dalen 1999), we believe this will only have a minor effect on the enduring citation impact of a Nobel Prize laureate. Fourth, various fields have different citation practices, leading to double counting in some instances (Klein and Chiang 2004).[12] Fifth, while the non-electronic SSCI database counts citations to books, manuscripts, and journals, the electronic Thompson ISI database counts only citations in articles published in its 1,950 (as of November 12, 2009) selected journals (Klein and Chiang 2004: 136). Klein and Chiang (2004: 136) argue that the selection of included journals is ideologically biased against classical liberalism. Davis (1998) shows that journals that share content with other academic fields are underrepresented in the Thompson ISI database.

In addition to the above difficulties, we observed further problems. First, we did not attempt to include references to Nobel Prize winners who misspelled their names because the number of misspelled names in academic publications is likely to be minor. In determining the citation counts for Nobel Laureates who share names with other researchers in the social sciences, we judged according to the citing articles and the cited articles to the best of our knowledge to minimize miscounts. Second, the electronic SSCI is skewed in favor of more recent scholars because it only counts citations for articles included in the Thompson ISI database published after 1980. For instance, Friedrich A. Hayek who did not publish any articles in Thompson ISI approved journals after 1980 shows zero citations from 1980–2008 in the electronic database, yet he receives 7,645 since 1980 in the non-electronic database over those dates. Therefore, even though Hayek received citations to his earlier work, the electronic database did not register them.

Results

Individually, mainline Nobel Laureates were cited more often than mainstream Laureates. In terms of electronic and non-electronic SSCI citations mainline Nobel Prize winners are more successful in maintaining an enduring impact on the social science profession than mainstream Nobel Prize winners. Table 2 presents the core results. On

Table 2

Descriptive Statistics

Non-electronic SSCI 1970–2007					
	Mean	Min	Max	Obs	Description
Mainline annual citations	287	0	1370	527	Annual citations of a mainline Nobel Prize winning economist
Mainstream annual citations	159	0	1643	1877	Annual citations of a mainstream Nobel Prize winning economist
Electronic SSCI 1980–2007					
	Mean	Min	Max	Obs	Description
Mainline annual citations	66	0	595	392	Annual citations of a mainline Nobel Prize winning economist
Mainstream annual citations	52	0	1178	1400	Annual citations of a mainstream Nobel Prize winning economist
General information					
	Mean	Min	Max	Obs	Description
Mainline year Nobel awarded	1994	1974	2009	14	Year in which the Nobel Prize was awarded to a mainline economist
Mainstream year Nobel awarded	1989	1969	2008	50	Year in which the Nobel Prize was awarded to a mainstream economist
Mainline shared Nobel	0.57	0	1	14	Dummy that takes on the value 1 if a mainline economist shared the Nobel Prize

Table 2 *Continued*

General information					
	Mean	Min	Max	Obs	Description
Mainstream shared Nobel	0.68	0	1	50	Dummy that takes on the value 1 if a mainstream economist shared the Nobel Prize
Mainline alphabetical rank	12	2	22	14	Number of the family name's first letter of a mainline economist in the Latin alphabet
Mainstream alphabetical rank	12.47	1	22	50	Number of the family name's first letter of a mainstream economist in the Latin alphabet

average, each mainline Nobel Laureate received 287 citations annually in the non-electronic SSCI over the period from 1970 to 2007. Over the same period, each mainstream Nobel Laureate received on average 159 citations per annum. Figure 1 compares the average annual non-electronic SSCI citations of mainline and mainstream Nobel Laureates from 1970 to 2007. Mainline economists also received more average annual citations in the electronic SSCI over the period from 1980 to 2007, shown in Figure 2. Mainline economists were on average cited 66 times, whereas mainstream economists were on average cited 52 times per year.

The non-electronic SSCI covers a broader range of outlets than the electronic SSCI does. It is therefore not surprising that both mainline and mainstream economists received more citations in the non-electronic than in the electronic SSCI. However, although on average mainline economists received more citations than mainstream economists in the non-electronic and the electronic SSCI, the relative gap is larger in the case of the non-electronic SSCI.[13] Per person, mainline economists received about 80 percent more average annual citations according to the non-electronic SSCI, whereas they only received

Figure 1

Mainline vs. Mainstream:
Nobel Laureates' Average Annual Non-Electronic SSCI Citations
1970–2007

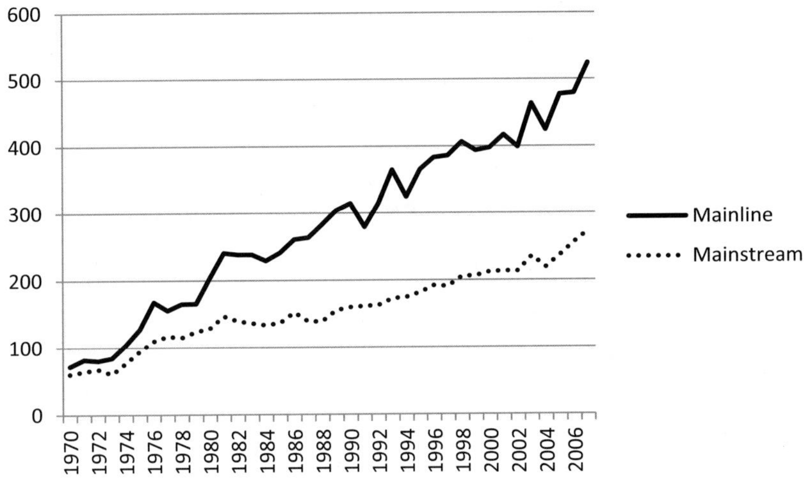

about 27 percent more annual citations according to the electronic SSCI. The results suggest that the impact of mainline Nobel Laureates is broader among the social sciences than the impact of mainstream Laureates.[14] Not only does the non-electronic SSCI cover references to books, whereas the electronic SSCI only covers references to journal articles, but the non-electronic SSCI also takes into account journals from a broader array of the social sciences. Although the effects are not separable, mainline economists seem to have received more references to their books and/or have been referred to by scholars from their own discipline of economics or bordering disciplines who publish in outlets that are not accounted for by the electronic SSCI.

We take a closer look at the citations of Nobel Prize winning economists and separate financial economists as well as economists whose major contributions lie in the field of econometrics. We illustrate the results in Figures 3 and 4. Figure 3 depicts the development of average annual non-electronic citations of the four identified groups

Figure 2

Mainline vs. Mainstream:
Nobel Laureates' Average Annual Electronic SSCI Citations
1980–2007

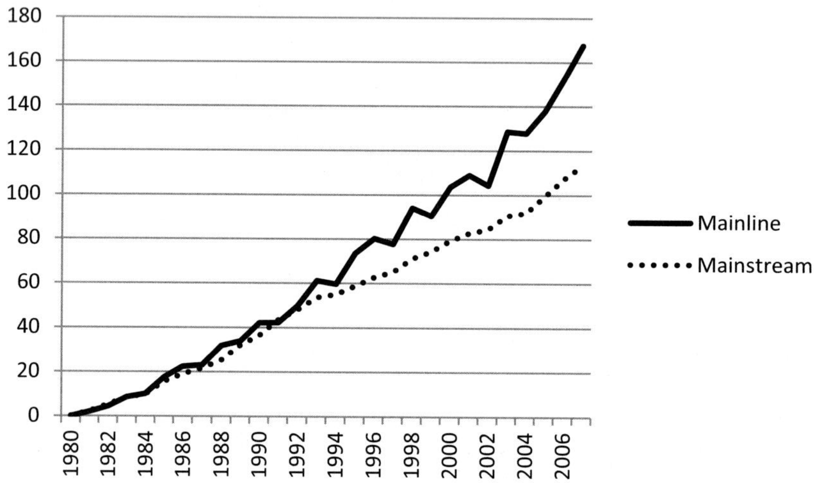

of economists—mainline, mainstream, financial economists—and econometricians. An individual member of the group of mainline economists over the period from 1970 to 2007 on average in each year received more citations than a member of any of the other three groups did. Figure 4 tells a different story. In Figure 4, the average annual electronic SSCI citations are depicted for the four groups. From the late 1980s onwards a member of the econometrician group on average received more citations than a member of any other group. Over the period from 1980 to 2007, mainline economists come in second. From this exhibition, we can conclude that the smaller gap between mainline and mainstream economists in the case of the electronic SSCI citations is driven by the members of the group of mainstream economists who received the Nobel Prize for their contributions in econometrics. It is not surprising that the econometricians' share of the total electronic SSCI citations is larger than their share of the total non-electronic SSCI citations. Econometricians are less likely to publish their findings in book form than other economists

Figure 3

Alternative Categorization
Nobel Laureates' Average Annual Non-Electronic SSCI Citations
1970–2007

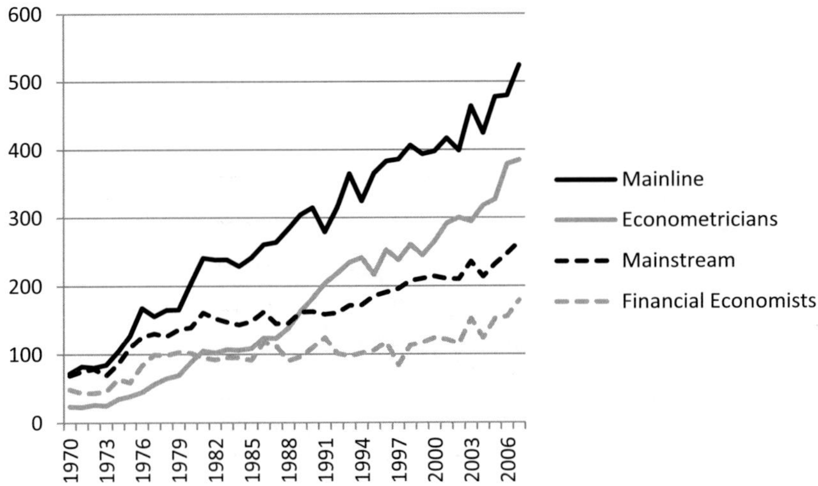

and members of other social science disciplines are less likely to refer to their work because in their work they rely less on quantitative empirical methods than economists.

According to the Nobel Prize rules, a Nobel Prize may be granted to up to three persons. The Nobel Prize Committee states that shared Prizes are just as honorable as a single prize. Shared prizes are awarded "when the contributions are the results of actual cooperative work," *or* when the contributors are so closely related that a sharing is important to demonstrate the connection and to be "'fair' to contributors" (Lindbeck 2007). Yet, historically, the profession and the recipients regard single Prizes to be more prestigious than shared Prizes. Table 2 shows that the percentage of mainline shared Nobel prizes, 57, was very similar to the number of shared prizes for mainstream economists, 68, suggesting that our results are not driven by these factors.

As mentioned in the third section of this article, the non-electronic SSCI only reports the first-mentioned author of an article. It is,

Figure 4

Alternative Categorization
Nobel Laureates' Average Annual Electronic SSCI Citations
1980–2007

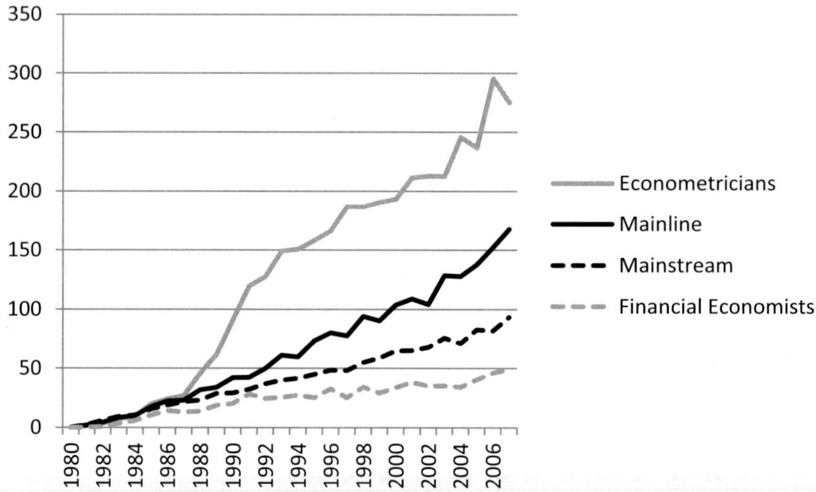

however, not the case that the large number of citations going to mainline economists in the non-electronic SSCI relative to the electronic SSCI, which credits all co-authors for an article, is owed to relatively many mainline economists with family names starting with letters that appear early in the alphabet. Figure 5 shows that over the period from 1970 to 2007 the average number of annual non-electronic SSCI citations was larger for a member of the group whose family names started with a letter between A and H than for a member of the remaining group of Laureates. However, there is no systematic difference between mainline and mainstream economists with respect to their family names' first letter's position in the alphabet. We attached numbers from 1 to 24 to letters from A to W and built the average for mainline and mainstream economists. Table 2 shows that the average is 12 for mainline economists and 12.42 for mainstream economists. This difference most likely did not cause the observed difference in the citation pattern between the two groups.

Figure 5

Nobel Laureates' Average Annual Non-Electronic SSCI Citations
Names starting with A-H vs. names starting with K-W
1970–2007

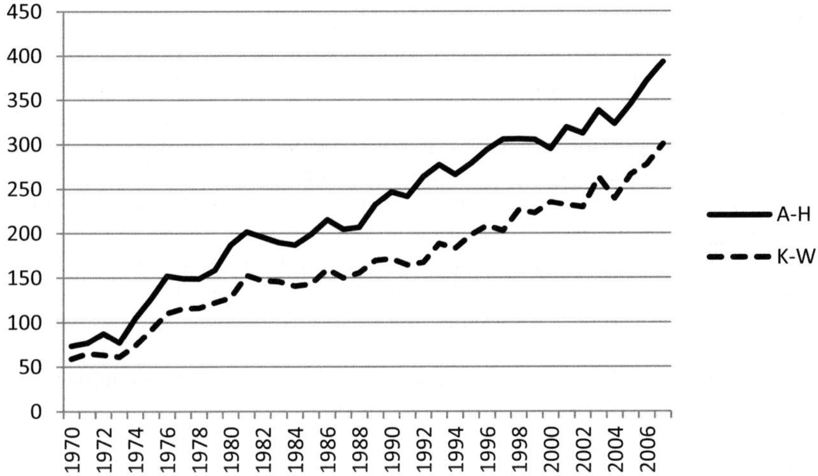

Conclusion

The expanding field of economics into many subfields may be considered a positive development for a maturing science. Yet, the close connection between economics and politics presents a temptation to alter the allocation of scholarly efforts to fashionable areas that tend to bring fame and prominence over scholarly pursuits that bring less personal accolades but advance the core propositions of the discipline.

We find that those Nobel Laureates who allocated their scholarly activities to advancing our understanding of the core ideas of the discipline, first advanced by Adam Smith and David Hume, are the scholars who have maintained the largest enduring impact on the social science profession as measured by the annual number of citations received.

Notes

1. Hayek (1948: 11) argues that it is a misconception to ascribe to Adam Smith and mainline scholars who have built upon his work the assumption that economic man is perfectly rational. In fact, it is quite the opposite, as Smith ([1759] 1976: 184; [1776] 1976: 456) stresses man in his very nature is self-interested, lazy, wasteful, and short-sighted. Hume ([1742] 1987: Part I, Essay VI) goes so far as to assume all men are knaves. As Hayek (1948: 11) describes it, ". . .the main point about which there can be little doubt is that [Adam] Smith's chief concern was not so much with what man might occasionally achieve when he was at his best but that he should have as little opportunity as possible to do harm when he was at his worst. It would scarcely be too much to claim that the main merit of the individualism which he and his contemporaries advocated is that is a system under which bad men can do least harm. It is a social system which does not depend for its functioning on our finding good men for running it, or on all men becoming better than they now are, but which makes use of men in all their given variety and complexity, sometimes good and sometimes bad, sometimes intelligent and more often stupid."

2. The focus of 20th-century mainstream economists on choice rather than exchange was accompanied by the convention to follow the examples set by Samuelson with respect to the acceptable form of theorizing—formal mathematics—and by Friedman with respect to the testing of economic hypotheses by using statistical techniques, instead of basing economic methodology on a philosophy of science (Boettke 2010).

3. Throughout the article, winners of the Sveriges Riksbank Prize in Economic Sciences in Memory of Alfred Nobel are referred to simply as "Nobel Laureates."

4. The Social Science Citation Index is a citation indexing service product of Thomas ISI. We used the annual paper editions from 1970–2007 in the Library of Congress.

5. Appendix 1 uses our data set to compare the relative contributions of Nobel Prize Laureates who were at institutions in the U.S. vs. foreign institutions.

6. Appendix 2 uses our data set to compare the relative contributions of extreme conceptual, moderate conceptual, and experimental Nobel Laureates according to Weinberg and Galenson's (2005) categorization.

7. Appendix 3 uses our data set to compare the relative contributions of Lindbeck's (1985) categories.

8. Appendix 4 uses our data set to compare the relative contributions of Karier's (2010) categories.

9. Kirzner (1965) argues that it was not Robbins' intention to place resource allocation decisions at the core of economics. Robbins (1932: 17–19) argues that essentially economics is not just the study of nonsocial behavior.

Robbins posits that "economic analysis has most utility in the exchange economy. It is unnecessary in the isolated economy."

10. For a general overview of Lakatos' work and its relation to economics, see Rizzo (1982).

11. For further support of the use of citations to measure a scholar's influence on the profession, see Downing and Stafford (1981: 220), who note that "while one might argue that citations from publications would also be biased, the bias is that of the profession and its journal editors and referees rather than of the investigator." Arguments in favor of citations as a measure of scholarly influence can also be found in Cole and Cole (1973), Laband and Sophocleus (1985), Davis and Papanek (1984), and Stigler, Stigler, and Friedland (1995). For a critical voice, see, for instance, Klein and Chiang (2004) and Medoff (1989), who argue that citations might be critical of the referenced work, either correcting errors or doubting the accuracy of the work, and therefore should not be included as positive citations. On the other hand, citation counts are possibly biased against important contribution that are incorporated into the profession and for which the originators of the idea are no longer cited (Stigler, Stigler, and Friedland 1995; Anderson, Levy, and Tollison 1989).

12. This is true of law reviews, meaning that economists that are cited heavily in law review journals may have inflated citations over economists cited in economic journals. Like many of the problems listed here, when dealing with a hand-counted citation database, or even the electronic database, attempting to adjust for citations in law reviews would require extensive efforts. Since the SSCI citations counts are the accepted measure of a scholar's impact in the profession, we merely adopt the standard practice for our analysis.

13. Appendix 5 provides the total non-electronic citations for the Nobel Laureates; Appendix 6 does the same for the electronic citations.

14. The graph presented in Appendix 7 suggests that the relative impact of mainline Nobel Laureates has been growing over the last decades. The share of annual total non-electronic and electronic citations received by mainline Nobel Laureates has been growing from roughly 25 percent to 35 percent since 1970 and from roughly 20 percent to 30 percent since 1981, respectively. Using OLS to regress the share of citations for mainline Laureates on the time trend suggests that the time trend is statistically significant at the 1 percent percent level for electronic and non-electronic citations. The same holds true when the share of mainline citations is transformed into logit form to account for the boundedness between 0 and 1 of the fraction. The regression results are not reported here. They can be provided by the authors upon request.

References

Acton, Lord (1904). *Letters of Lord Acton to Mary Gladstone*, ed. Herbert Paul. London: Macmillan Company.

Alexander, J. C., and R. H. Mabry. (1994). "Relative Significance of Journals, Authors, and Articles Cited in Financial Research." *Journal of Finance* 49: 697–712.

Anderson, G. M., D. M. Levy, and R. D. Tollison. (1989). "The Half-Life of Dead Economists." *Canadian Journal of Economics* 22(1): 174–83.

Boettke, P. J. (2007). "Liberty vs. Power in Economic Policy in the 20th and 21st Centuries," *Journal of Private Enterprise* 22(2): 7–36.

——. (2010). "Twentieth-Century Economic Methodology." In *21st Century Economics: A Reference Handbook*. Ed. Rhona C. Free, pp. 33–44. Thousand Oaks, CA: SAGE Publications, Inc.

——. (2011). "Economics for Yesterday, Today and Tomorrow." *Journal of Private Enterprise* 26(1): 1–14.

—— (2012). *Living Economics*. Oakland, CA: Independent Institute.

Boettke, Peter J., Peter T. Leeson, and Daniel J. Smith. (2008). "The Evolution of Economics: Where We Are and How We Got Here." *Long Term View* 7(1): 14–22.

Buchanan, J. M. (1964). "What Should Economists Do?" *Southern Economic Journal* 30(1): 213–222.

——. (2001). "Game Theory, Mathematics and Economics." *Journal of Economic Methodology* 8(1): 27–32.

Chung, K. H., R. Cox, and A. A. Okunade. (1993). "Publishing Behavior of Individuals and Most Prolific Authors in the Economics Literature." *Quarterly Journal of Business and Economics* 32(3): 32–42.

Coase, Ronald H. (1978). "Economics and Contiguous Disciplines." *Journal of Legal Studies* 7(2): 201–211.

Cole, J. R., and S. Cole. (1973). *Social Stratification in Science*. Chicago: University of Chicago Press.

Davis, J. B. (1998). "Problems in Using the Social Science Citation Index to Rank Economics Journals." *American Economist* 42(2): 59–64.

Davis, P., and G. F. Papanek. (1984). "Faculty Ratings of Major Economics Departments by Citations." *American Economic Review* 74(2): 225–230.

Diamond, A. M. (1988). "Citation Counts for Nobel Prize Winners in Economics." *History of Economics Science Bulletin* 10: 67–70.

Downing, P. B., and E. A. Stafford. (1981). "Citations as an Indicator of Classic Works and Major Contributions in Social Choice." *Public Choice* 37(2): 219–230.

Hayek, F. A. (1937). "Economics and Knowledge." *Economica* 4(13): 33–54.

——. (1948). *Individualism and Economic Order*. Chicago, IL: Chicago University Press.

——. (1988). *The Fatal Conceit: The Errors of Socialism.* Chicago: University of Chicago Press.

Hume, D. ([1742] 1987). "Of the Independency of Parliament." In *Essays, Moral, Political, and Literary.* Ed. Eugene F. Miller, I.VI. Indianapolis, IN: Liberty Fund, Inc.

Karier, T. (2010). *Intellectual Capital: Forty Years of the Nobel Prize in Economics.* New York: Cambridge University Press.

Kelly, M. A., and S. Bruestle. (2010). "Trend of Subjects Published in Economics Journals 1969–2007." *Economic Inquiry* Mar: 1–16.

Kirzner, I. (1965). "What Economists Do." *Southern Economic Journal* 31(3): 257–261.

Klein, D., and E. Chiang. (2004). "The Social Science Citation Index: A Black Box—With an Ideological Bias?" *Economic Journal Watch* 1(1):134–165.

Kreps, D. (1997). "Economics: The Current Position." *Daedalus* 126(1): 59–85.

Laband, D. N., and J. P. Sophocleus. (1985). "Revealed Preference for Economic Journals: Citations as Dollar Votes." *Public Choice* 46(3): 317–324.

Landes, W. M., and R. A. Posner. (1976). "Legal Precedent: A Theoretical and Empirical Analysis," *Journal of Law and Economics* 19(2): 249–307.

Lindbeck, Assar. (1985). "The Prize in Economic Science in Memory of Alfred Nobel." *Journal of Economic Literature* 23(1): 37–56.

——. (2007). "The Sveriges Riksbank Prize in Economic Sciences in Memory of Alfred Nobel 1969–2007." *Nobelprize.org.* Available. Http: <http://www.nobelprize.org/nobel_prizes/economics/articles/lindbeck/> (accessed August 20 2011).

Medoff, M. A. (1989). "The Ranking of Economists." *Journal of Economic Education* 20(4): 405–415.

North, D. C. (1994). "Douglas C. North." In *Lives of the Laureates: Twenty-Three Nobel Economists.* Eds. William Breit, and Barry T. Hirsch, pp. 209–222. Cambridge, Massachusetts: MIT Press.

Nozick, R. (1974). *Anarchy, State and Utopia.* New York: Basic Books, Inc.

Ostrom, E. (1997). "A Behavioral Approach to the Rational Choice Theory of Collective Action." *American Political Science Review* 92(1): 1–22.

——. (2010). "Beyond Markets and States: Polycentric Governance of Complex Economic Systems." *American Economic Review* 100(3): 641–672.

Rizzo, Mario. (1982). "Mises and Lakatos: A Reformulation of Austrian Methodology." In *Method, Process, and Austrian Economics: Essays in Honor of Ludwig von Mises.* Ed. Israel M. Kirzner, pp. 53–74. Lexington, MA: D.C. Heath and Company.

Robbins, Lionel C. (1932). *An Essay on the Nature and Significance of Economic Science.* London: MacMillian and Co.

Skarbek, David B. (2009). "F.A. Hayek's Influence on Nobel Prize Winners." *Review of Austrian Economics* 22(1): 109–112.

Smith, Adam. ([1759] 1976). *The Theory of Moral Sentiments.* Eds. D. D. Faphael and A. L. Macfie. Indianapolis, IN: Liberty Fund, Inc.

——. ([1776] 1976). *An Inquiry into the Nature and Causes of the Wealth of Nations*, Vol. 1. Eds. R. H. Campbell and A. S. Skinner. Indianapolis, IN: Liberty Fund, Inc.

Smith, V. (1974). "Economic Theory and Its Discontents." *American Economic Review* 64(2): 320–322.

Stigler, G. J. ([1985] 2009). "George J. Stigler." In *Lives of the Laureates: Twenty-Three Nobel Economists.* Eds. William Breit and Barry T. Hirsch, pp. 79–93. Cambridge, MA: MIT Press.

Stigler, G. J., Stephen M. Stigler, and Claire Friedland. (1995). "The Journals of Economics." *Journal of Political Economy* 103(2): 331–359.

Ullmann-Margalit, E. (1978). "Invisible-Hand Explanations." *Synthese* 39(2): 263–291.

van Dalen, H. P. (1999). "The Golden Age of Nobel Economists." *American Economist* 43(2): 19–35.

Weinberg, B. A., and D. W. Galenson. (2005). "Creative Careers: The Life Cycles of Nobel Laureates in Economics." NBER Working Paper No. W11799.

Williamson, O. E. (2002). "The Theory of the Firm as Governance Structure: From Choice to Contract." *Journal of Economic Perspectives* 16(3): 171–195.

Appendix 1:
Citation Impact of Nobel Laureates in Economics at United States Institutions vs. Foreign Institutions (Non-Electronic SSCI Database)

United States				Foreign
Akerlof	Kahneman	Modigliani	Smith	Allais
Arrow	Klein	Mundell	Solow	Aumann
Becker	Koopmans	Myerson	Spence	Frisch
Buchanan	Krugman	Nash	Stigler	Haavelmo
Coase	Kuznets	North	Stiglitz	Hicks
Debreu	Kydland	Ostrom	Tobin	Kantorovich
Engle	Leontief	Phelps	Vickrey	Meade
Fogel	Lewis	Prescott	Williamson	Mirrlees
Friedman	Lucas	Samuelson		Myrdal
Granger	Markowitz	Schelling		Ohlin
Harsanyi	Maskin	Scholes		Selten
Hayek	McFadden	Schultz		Sen
Heckman	Merton	Sharpe		Stone
Hurwicz	Miller	Simon		Tinbergen

Note: We classify an economist as working in the United States if, at the time of being awarded the Nobel Prize, he or she was working at an institution in the United States.

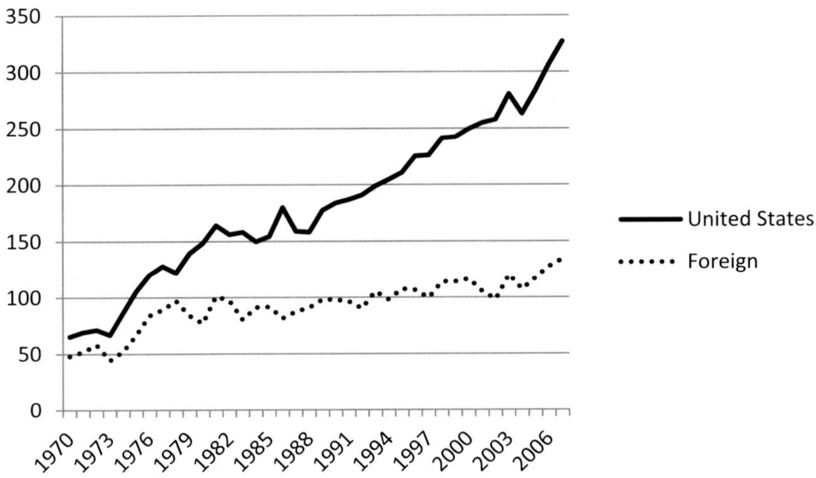

Appendix 2:
Weinberg and Galenson's Categorization
(Non-Electronic SSCI Database)

Extreme Conceptual	Moderate Conceptual		Experimental
Arrow	Buchanan	Miller	Fogel
Debreu	Coase	Modigliani	Kuznets
Frisch	Friedman	Ohlin	Myrdal
Haavelmo	Hayek	Simon	North
Harsanyi	Klein	Stigler	Schultz
Hicks	Leontief	Stone	
Samuelson	Lewis	Tinbergen	
Solow	Markowitz	Tobin	
	Meade	Vickrey	

Note: We use our non-electronic SSCI database to compare the relative citation impact of Galenson and Weinberg's (2005) classification of economists into three groups, extreme conceptual, moderate conceptual, and experimental. They classify economists who work inductively as experimental economists and those who work deductively as conceptual economists. Their classification of Nobel Prize winning economists is reproduced below. The chart below shows that inductive economists, on average, have had less of a citation impact on the profession than deductive economists.

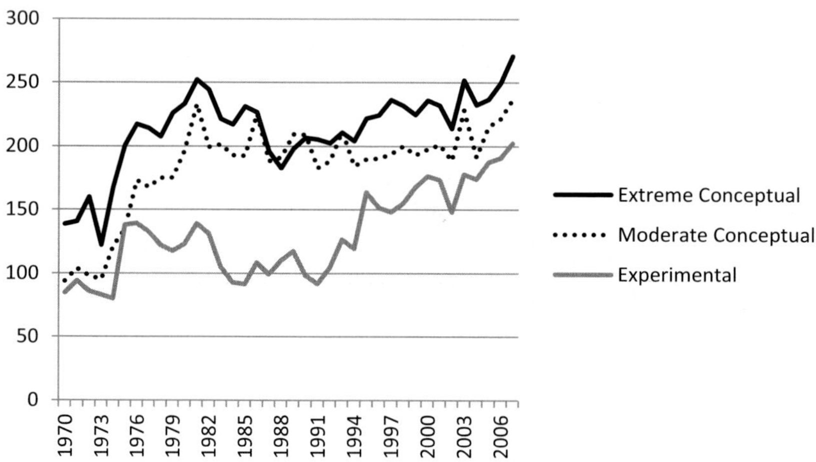

Appendix 3:
Lindbeck's Categorization (Non-Electronic SSCI Database)

Theoretical Contributions Concerning Specific Aspects or Sectors of the Economy	Development and Application of Powerful New Methods of Economic Analysis
Friedman	Frisch
Lewis	Kantorovich
Meade	Koopmans
Ohlin	Leontief
Schultz	Stone
Simon	Tinbergen
Stigler	
Tobin	
Non-Formalized Innovative Thinking	**More Nearly "Pure" Empirical Research**
Hayek	Klein
Myrdal	Kuznets
General Economic Theory	
Arrow	
Debreu	
Hicks	
Samuelson	

Note: We use the non-electronic SSCI database to examine the relative citation impact of Lindbeck's (1985) classification of Nobel Prize winning economists into five groups, those who made contributions to general economic theory, theoretical contributions concerning specific aspects or sectors of the economy, powerful new methods of economic analysis, pure empirical research, and non-formalized innovative thinking. The chart below shows that those economists that Lindbeck classifies as working in general economic theory, theoretical contributions, and non-formalized innovative thinking have a greater citation impact than those working in pure empirical methods or powerful new methods of economic analysis.

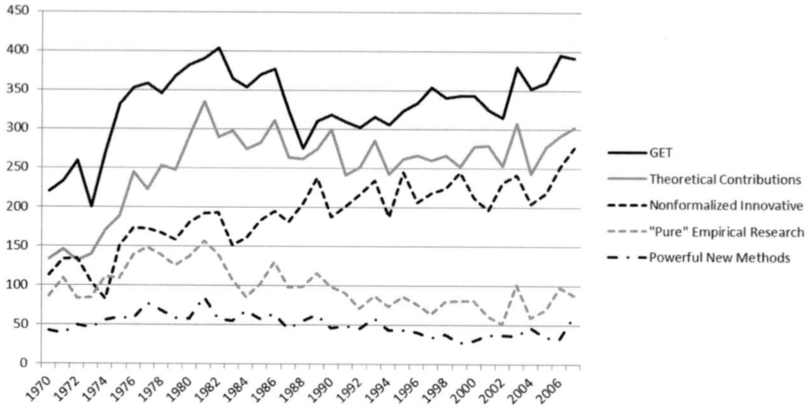

Appendix 4: Karier's Categorization (Non-Electronic SSCI Database)

Classical Revival	History and Institutions	Micro: The Chicago School	Free Market Economics
Kydland	Fogel	Becker	Buchanan
Lucas	North	Coase	Friedman
Phelps	Ostrom	Schultz	Hayek
Prescott	Williamson	Stigler	
More Micro	**A World View**	**Game Geeks**	**Number Guys**
Hicks	Krugman	Aumann	Engle
Mirrlees	Lewis	Harsanyi	Frisch
Smith	Meade	Hurwicz	Granger
Vickrey	Mundell	Maskin	Haavelmo
	Ohlin	Myerson	Heckman
	Sen	Nash	McFadden
		Schelling	Tinbergen
		Selten	

Appendix 4 *Continued*

Behaviorists	Inventors	Stock Market Casino	Keynesians
Kahneman	Kantorovich	Markowitz	Klein
Simon	Koopmans	Merton	Modigliani
Spence	Kuznets	Miller	Myrdal
Stiglitz	Leontief	Scholes	Samuelson
	Stone	Sharpe	Solow
			Tobin

General Equilibrium
Allais
Arrow
Debreu

Note: We use our non-electronic SSCI database of Nobel Prize winners to compare the citation impact of the 13 groups that Karier (2010) split economists into: behaviorists, history and institutions, micro: the Chicago School, free market economics, number guys, general equilibrium, a world view, classical revival, Keynesians, game geeks, stock market casino, more micro, and inventors.

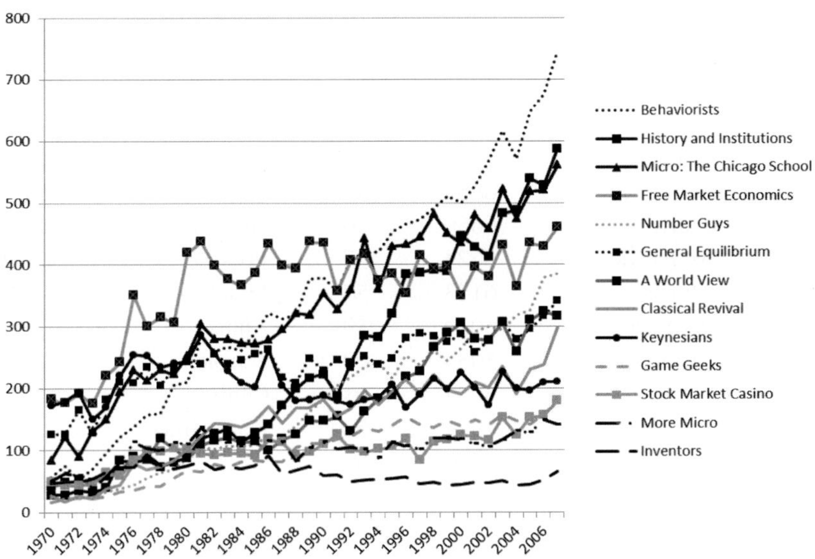

Appendix 5:
Nobel Laureates' Total Non-Electronic SSCI Citations 1970–2007

1	Becker	24148	33	Sharpe	4519
2	Kahneman	23865	34	Debreu	4468
3	Simon	23198	35	Nash	4018
4	Friedman	22649	36	Aumann	3911
5	Arrow	21512	37	Phelps	3868
6	Williamson	20675	38	Markowitz	3466
7	Samuelson	17221	39	Leontief	3422
8	Sen	16575	40	Schultz	3412
9	Lucas	14101	41	Miller	3307
10	Heckman	13421	42	Mundell	3042
11	Stigler	13205	43	Lewis	3039
12	Krugman	11070	44	Myerson	3025
13	Engle	10993	45	Tinbergen	2887
14	Stiglitz	10642	46	Kydland	2788
15	Buchanan	10003	47	Klein	2762
16	Coase	9563	48	Fogel	2724
17	Granger	8848	49	Koopmans	2704
18	Hayek	8382	50	Selten	2636
19	Tobin	7954	51	Spence	2619
20	North	7790	52	Meade	2560
21	Hicks	7183	53	Maskin	2368
22	Solow	7105	54	Vickrey	2123
23	Schelling	6852	55	Mirrlees	1967
24	Merton	6659	56	Hurwicz	1760
25	McFadden	6623	57	Prescott	1729
26	Myrdal	6153	58	Frisch	1597
27	Akerlof	6026	59	Allais	1592
28	Modigliani	5953	60	Scholes	1377
29	Harsanyi	5014	61	Ohlin	927
30	Ostrom	4914	62	Haavelmo	581
31	Smith	4690	63	Stone	414
32	Kuznets	4682	64	Kantorovich	380

Appendix 6:
Nobel Laureates' Total Electronic SSCI Citations
1980–2007

1	Kahneman	12570	33	Fogel	412
2	Engle	10731	34	Spence	380
3	Granger	7725	35	Schelling	357
4	Stiglitz	7470	36	Stigler	329
5	Lucas	5849	37	Scholes	312
6	Heckman	4867	38	Coase	283
7	Simon	4335	39	Klein	250
8	Becker	4119	40	Markowitz	197
9	Krugman	4099	41	Sharpe	145
10	Williamson	3311	42	Allais	139
11	Prescott	3202	43	Phelps	124
12	Maskin	2979	44	Leontief	115
13	Smith	2581	45	Lewis	112
14	Akerlof	2417	46	Mirrlees	100
15	Myerson	2269	47	Debreu	91
16	Ostrom	2151	48	Hurwicz	64
17	McFadden	1876	49	Vickrey	63
18	Merton	1601	50	Tinbergen	61
19	Kydland	1423	51	Schultz	51
20	North	1161	52	Meade	36
21	Miller	1072	53	Mundell	27
22	Solow	1025	54	Hicks	19
23	Arrow	1009	55	Koopmans	18
24	Aumann	837	56	Frisch	7
25	Selten	745	57	Kuznets	7
26	Friedman	721	58	Nash	7
27	Samuelson	614	59	Ohlin	5
28	Harsanyi	543	60	Haavelmo	3
29	Buchanan	487	61	Kantorovich	1
30	Tobin	470	62	Hayek	0
31	Modigliani	417	63	Myrdal	0
32	Stone	416	64	Sen	0

Appendix 7:
Mainline vs. Mainstream
Nobel Laureates' Total Annual Non-Electronic SSCI Citations
1970–2007

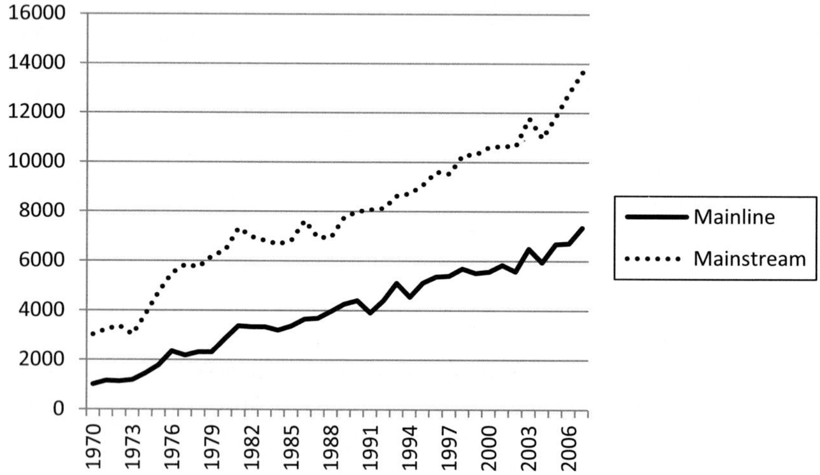

Appendix 8:
Mainline vs. Mainstream
Nobel Laureates' Total Annual Electronic SSCI Citations
1980–2007

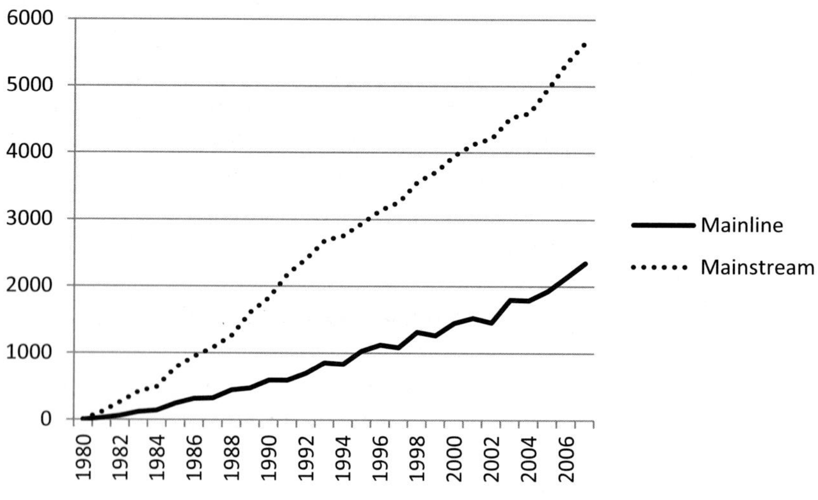

Appendix 9:
Mainline vs. Mainstream
Mainline Share of Total Electronic and Non-Electronic Citations
1970–2007

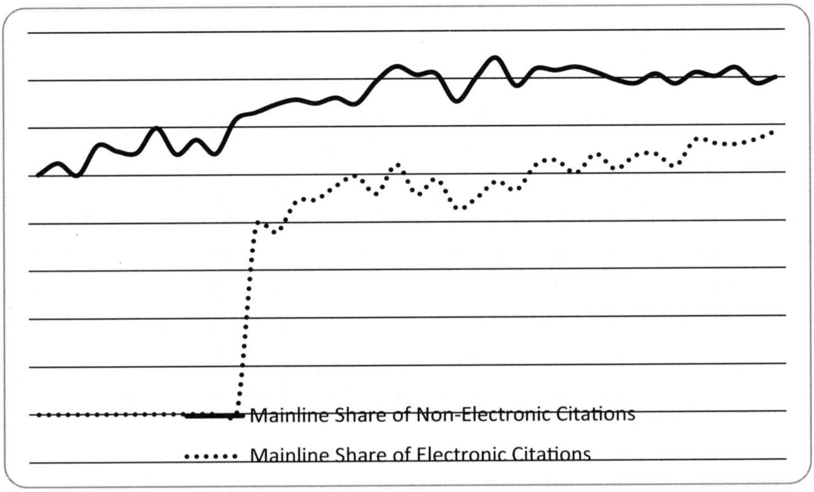

The Forsaken-Liberty Syndrome: Looking at Published Judgments to Say Whether Economists Reach a Conclusion

By DANIEL B. KLEIN*

ABSTRACT. Do economists reach a conclusion on a given policy issue? One way to answer the question is to survey economists at large. Another is to look at the published judgments of economists who have gone on the record. Relative to an anonymous survey, going on the record makes for much greater accountability, and presumably more personal responsibility. I discuss 11 studies of economists' published judgments. Several of them show greater support for liberalization than found among economists at large. This is offered as evidence of what I call the forsaken-liberty syndrome. I discuss the nature of this test of such syndrome and point to some of the larger questions to which it relates.

In this article I discuss looking at published judgments to address the question of whether economists reach a conclusion on a policy issue. That task speaks to a larger matter, which I call the forsaken-liberty syndrome. But first I remark on how the article relates to the theme of this *AJES* special issue, *the contributions of dissident economists.*

Dissidence is exemplified by the miscreant who goes against the status quo, or even challenges it. The status quo is the context of our experience, knowledge, talk, and action. It is our usual point of departure. It is naturally focal, and people naturally give presumption to the status quo: The burden of proof is placed on the one proposing to reform it.

When it dominates, the presumption of the status quo casts as dissident anyone who discounts that presumption and instead holds

*George Mason University, dklein@gmu.edu.

Written for a special issue of the *American Journal of Economics and Sociology* on the contributions of dissident economists, edited by Daniel Sutter.

Acknowledgments: For valuable comments I thank Jason Briggeman, Tyler Cowen, and Robert Whaples and for proofreading, Hannah Mead.

American Journal of Economics and Sociology, Vol. 71, No. 5 (November, 2012).

up some other. The type of dissident economist that is relevant for this article is the classical liberal economist, who gives the presumption to the liberty principle. To such a liberal, policies that contravene the liberty principle should bear the burden of proof, even if they are the status quo. Adam Smith and Jeremy Bentham provide illustration.

Even after cataloging all the exceptions, Jacob Viner wrote: "There is no possible room for doubt, however, that Smith in general believed that there was, to say the least, *a strong presumption* against government activity beyond its fundamental duties of protection against its foreign foes and maintenance of justice" (Viner 1927: 219, italics added).

One of Smith's exceptions was his endorsement of the status-quo ceiling on interest rates. Smith assumed the burden of proof, but not to Bentham's satisfaction. In *Defence of Usury*, Bentham writes to Smith:

> On this occasion, were it any individual antagonist I had to deal with, my part would be a smooth and easy one. "You, who fetter contracts; you, who lay restraints on the liberty of man, it is for you" (I should say) "to assign a reason for your doing so." That contracts in general ought to be observed, is a rule, the propriety of which, no man was ever yet found wrong-headed enough to deny: if this case is one of the exceptions (for some doubtless there are) which the safety and welfare of every society require should be taken out of that general rule, in this case, as in all those others, it lies upon him, who alledges the necessity of the exception, to produce a reason for it. . . .
>
> Should it be my fortune to gain any advantage over you [that is, Adam Smith], it must be with weapons which you have taught me to wield, and with which you yourself have furnished me . . . [A]ll the great standards of truth, which can be appealed to in this line, owe, as far as I can understand, their establishment to you . . . (Bentham 2008: 68)

Thus Bentham tells Smith: You have taught us the presumption of liberty; you have made an exception in this case; I will show that your attempt to meet the burden of proof fails. Bentham's critique is glorious and eventually carried the day; lore has it that Smith conceded the merit of Bentham's case (see the Preface to Bentham 2008).

There was a time when the presumption of liberty rose up to challenge the presumption of the status quo. Economists were once closely identified with the liberal presumption. Frédéric Bastiat (1964: 109) wrote: "the economists' principle implies *liberty*." Ludwig von Mises (1966: 67) said: "[E]conomics as such is a challenge to the conceit of those in power."

But the character of economists has changed a lot since the days of Smith, Bentham, and Bastiat. Now, in the United States, the ratio of professional economists who vote Democratic to those who vote Republican is about 2.5 to 1, and perhaps only about 10 percent of professional economists show consistent support for free-market policy positions (Klein and Stern 2007). It is fair to say that economics has fallen back to the presumption of the status quo.

In its approach to the question, "Do economists reach a conclusion?", this article deals indirectly with research of a great many economists. Many of those economists are ones who have examined a status-quo policy and judged in favor of liberalization. The analysis often works from a presumption of liberty, and bolsters it. This paper, then, treats of dissident economists in the sense that it highlights work suggesting that certain status-quo contraventions of liberty fail to meet the burden of proof.

How Should We Decide Whether Economists Reach a Conclusion?

> Indeed, the economist is rapidly becoming the stock butt for popular jest. "All the economists in the world if put end to end would not reach . . . a conclusion."
>
> Barbara Wootton (1938: 14)

The ambitious hope would be that economists judged alike on all things economic, but we shall humbly take one policy issue at a time. One way to decide whether economists agree on a particular policy issue is to survey economists at large, for example, from the membership of the American Economic Association. Many such U.S. surveys have been done—some since 2000 include Fuller and Geide-Stevenson (2003), Klein and Stern (2005), Whaples (2006, 2009), Davis et al. (2011), and May and Whaples (forthcoming). On a few issues, such as international trade, economists overwhelmingly support a liberal position. And economists are considerably more liberal (used throughout this article in the Gladstonean sense) than academics in other social-science and humanities fields (Klein and Stern 2005: 283). On most issues, however, economists are quite mixed. Bearing in mind that monkeys throwing darts would generate a uniform distribution, one is struck by the fact that Likert-scale results quite often show some U-shapedness (or lack of single-peakedness), revealing cleavages between interventionists and liberals. In fact, economics shows less consensus on policy than do the other social sciences, for the simple reason that the other fields harbor so few conservatives and libertarians (Klein and Stern 2005: 286).

People tap bartenders for beer and economists for economic opinion. Economists are thought to be more knowledgeable and more responsible in forming judgments. But how well do surveys target knowledge and incentivize responsibility? The random economist who answers a survey does not necessarily know much about the issues asked, and he has little incentive to judge responsibly. He sits alone in his office. The survey is anonymous, so there is little accountability. His name is not attached to his responses. He is not open to challenges to his responses. Would you drink a beer that was delivered in some analogous fashion?

There is something to be said for anonymity, however. In journalism, reporters sometimes prefer that sources speak in confidence and remain unidentified because the veil of anonymity makes their communication *more* telling. The source can be more candid precisely because he does not have to face repercussions of going on the record. The same logic would apply for the refereeing of submissions to a scholarly journal.

As for an economist writing or speaking publicly on a policy issue, he, too, may feel certain incentives that lead him to "falsify" his beliefs (Kuran 1995), such as incentives of political opportunism, academic prudence, and pandering in general. There is, however, an important difference between the case of the journalist's source and the economist who speaks publicly: The impulse to speak comes from the economist himself, whereas a source related to a news story is tapped directly by the journalist.

A new development helps us to think about the distinction between "on-record" and "at-large" views of economists, and precisely because this new development straddles the two. At the University of Chicago, the Booth School of Business has created a fixed yet ongoing panel of 37 economists to respond to survey-type questions, on the record. The panel is part of the school's Initiative on Global Markets, and is here referred to as the IGM Panel. The IGM Panel is an example in which each panelist, such as Claudia Goldin, responds on the record. On the other hand, the panelist is being tapped on questions that may have nothing to do with her research, and about which she may not be particularly knowledgeable (though she may do research prior to answering the question), so in that respect is it like a survey of economists at large. The self-sorting aspect of normal on-record judgments does not apply for the IGM Panel.

I think that on-record scholarly judgments remain a special way to target knowledge and responsibility. When an economist steps forward to publish a judgment on a policy issue, he does so because he thinks he has something to add, and he attaches his name to the statement. He opens himself up to challenge. Such circumstances usually impel greater care. Moreover, the self-sorting means that the on-record economists are not a random sample of economists at large. All this is *not* meant to suggest that stepping forward and going on the record means getting it right, only that judgment emerging from that combination is generally better than judgment solicited by others and rendered in seclusion and anonymity.

In this article, the question that really ends up being the one that matters is this: How strong are the forces that impel an economist to step forward and publish a judgment *that is more pro-liberalization than he really believes?* I do not claim that such forces are entirely non-existent, but I think they are small enough in relation to the healthy incentives to justify the approach pursued here.

The Forsaken-Liberty Syndrome

Do we find discrepancies between the two sorts of tests? Yes, sometimes we do.

To my mind, the best illustration of the discrepancy is the comparison of results on the issue of the control of pharmaceuticals by the Food and Drug Administration. When randomly sampled AEA members were asked their position on "Pharmaceutical market regulation by the FDA," the response distribution was very preponderantly on the side of "support," rather than "oppose."[1] But an analysis of the published judgments by economists on the core FDA issues shows that such judgments very preponderantly favor liberalization (Klein 2008: 318–324). I believe that the FDA case exemplifies a syndrome: certain interventions that are hallowed and important to statist ethos and mythos are wrongheaded and fail to meet the liberal burden of proof; a substantial majority of economists are at the political center or the Democratic left, and their thinking and survey responses go along with such interventions; meanwhile such economists, with a few exceptions, are *not* willing to go on record with support for such interventions because justification is so poor, and that means that the judgments that do go on record come from economists who are willing to stray from such ethos and mythos.

Having the hunch of such syndrome, the editors of the journal called *Econ Journal Watch*, of which I am the chief editor, decided to cultivate and publish original studies under the heading "Do Economists Reach a Conclusion?" Eleven papers have been completed. The studies are not so much a review of the literature as a review of policy judgments expressed by economists. The reasoning behind such judgments gets treated, but the central tasks are to interpret, organize, and report the judgments. The 11 policy topics are: sports subsidies, the FDA, organ liberalization, rent control, drug policy, postal reform, medical licensing, taxi deregulation, rail transit, road pricing, and household and municipal recycling.

Here I do not summarize each of the papers but rather discuss the broader questions to which the set might speak. Does the set serve as meta-evidence of a forsaken-liberty syndrome wherein liberalization finds more consistent support among on-record economists than at-large economists? I abbreviate "Do Economists Reach a Conclusion" as DERAC, and speak of the 11 studies as the DERAC papers.[2] Table 1 provides information about the 11 studies.

After describing the methods of the DERAC papers and the apparent results of our test, I then turn back and offer some ruminations on the whole idea of such a test.

Table 1

Eleven *EJW* Papers on Whether Economists Reach a Conclusion

	Issue	Authors	Pub. date	A liberalization preponderance among on-record economists?	Data on at-large economists	Are the on-record economists more pro-liberalization than at-large economists?
*Three issues on which on-record and at-large economists seem to be **about the same** and to favor liberalization*						
1	Sports subsidies	Dennis Coates and Brad R. Humphreys	Sept 08	Strong yes	Whaples 06	About the same
2	Rent control	Blair Jenkins	Jan 09	Pretty strong yes	IGM Panel	Presumably about the same
3	Road pricing	Robin Lindsey	May 06	Strong agreement on pricing, but not other issues	IGM Panel	Presumably about the same
*Three issues on which on-record economists seem to be **significantly more supportive** of liberalization than at-large economists*						
4	FDA	Daniel Klein	Sept 08	Strong yes	Klein and Stern 05; Davis et al. 11	Yes
5	Medical licensing	Shirley Svorny	Aug 04	Fairly strong yes	Whaples 09; Davis et al. 11; IGM Panel	Yes
6	Postal reform	Rick Geddes	Apr 04	Fairly strong yes	Whaples 06	Yes

Two issues on which on-record economists seem to be ***mildly more supportive*** *of liberalization than at-large economists*						
7	Organ liberalization	Jon Diesel	Sept 10	Pretty strong yes	Whaples 09; Davis et al. 11	Yes, mildly
8	Drug policy	Mark Thornton	Apr 04	Fairly strong yes	Whaples 06; Klein and Stern 05; Davis et al. 11; IGM Panel	Yes, mildly
Two issues on which we do not know about at-large economists						
9	Taxi deregulation	Adian Moore and Ted Balaker	Jan 06	Fairly strong yes		Unknown
10	Rail transit	Ted Balaker and C.J. Kim	Sept 06	Qualified yes		Unknown
An issue on which on-record economists do not "reach a conclusion"						
11	Household and municipal recycling	Matthew Gunter	Jan 07	No	Whaples 09	Unsure, perhaps the same

Methods of the 11 DERAC Papers

The 11 papers share a common approach, with some variation, of course. The main facets follow in bold type:

Defining "economist." The papers generally count an author as an "economist" if *any* of the following criteria are met: he has a postgraduate degree in economics; he has taught college or university economics; he has been employed in a job with "economist" in the title; he has published more than incidentally in professional economics journals.

Defining the issue and the positions on the issue. Each policy topic has particularities that might suggest a variety of positions. Even the experts might disagree on how best to formulate "the issue." The authors of the DERAC papers find sensible ways of distinguishing positions. In most cases, the issue lends itself to formulation in terms of liberalization, that is, a relaxation of restrictions on the freedom of contract (for example, licensing laws) or on freedom in the use of private property (for example, drug laws). Sometimes the lines of property and consent are not so clear, notably in the issue of organ policy when economists support reforms toward "presumed consent" and "mandated choice." One might also use the term "liberalization" to include the reduction of tax-financed subsidies, for example, of sports or rail transit. The study that least well fits a liberalization formulation is the one that focuses on road pricing (Lindsey 2006), although retrofitting freeways with road pricing might relieve taxpayers somewhat, as well as put the freeway in a better position to be privatized. Perhaps the broad idea is better captured by *degovernmentalization*, but I stick with liberalization.

Method of canvassing for published judgments. The canvassing method varies among the papers, some confining the scope to scholarly literature, some including anything written by an economist. But the DERAC authors always describe their canvassing method. Svorny (2004), Geddes (2004), Lindsey (2006), and Coates and Humphreys (2008) are authorities on the treated topic, and they focus on the scholarly material of economists working on the topic. Lindsey (2006), Gunter (2007), Jenkins (2009), and Diesel (2010) start with Econlit searches and either fan out systematically or supplement in various ways, sometimes effectively scooping up everything they find. The papers that most freely include popular as well as scholarly sources—but all written by an economist—are Thornton (2004), Gunter (2007), Klein (2008), and Diesel (2010). I do not think that readers should suspect cherry-picking or opportunistic inclusion and exclusion. Even though the DERAC authors are themselves generally liberal, they are interested in spotlighting and examining the judgments and arguments in favor of intervention. In some cases, the study is pursued and the results turn out other than the DERAC author anticipated—a notable example is Gunter (2007) on household and municipal recycling, which finds, contrary to the author's expectation, that there is no consensus. Worries of opportunistic inclusion or exclusion should also be allayed by the "open-source" aspects of the discourse: if a reader were to find that a DERAC author had omitted relevant economists, that reader could bring it to the attention of the journal. Moreover, every article in *Econ Journal Watch* is stamped with a link that enables readers to comment directly on that article online. Thus far, no charges of opportunistic inclusion or exclusion have been aimed at any of the DERAC articles. The agenda of *Econ Journal Watch* entails standing up for the broad verities of liberal economics, but it also entails showing the failure of the economics profession to do so. The journal has no proclivity to make the profession out to be more liberal than it is. The extent and nature of the problem needs to be assessed as accurately as possible.

On "judgment": The object judged of. With an issue formulated in terms of vying positions, the paramount object for judgment would be a position on the issue. But a treated author often does not clearly identify a position on the issue, much less express a judgment of it. He may, however, treat of various signal factors that would figure into a judgment on a position, such as whether rent control reduces housing supply or affects housing quality. DERAC authors are careful to clarify the object judged of, and are careful not to read judgment of a factor as something wider than it is.

On "judgment": Reading the author's message. Instead of saying, "The government should abolish rent control," the economist might say, "Abolishing rent control would improve social welfare." Or he might speak to only certain factors in the issue. But one hopes that economic analysis is carried out on an understanding that the author treats of the things that are most important to the issue, and we use that understanding to infer the author's drift. Also, we read the author's work comprehensively, to see qualifications and assess the balance. DERAC authors assess the vagueness or clarity of a judgment, sometimes even schematically (Klein 2008; Diesel 2010: 328)—somewhat like the IGM Panel, which asks its 37 panelists to specify the confidence they have in their response. Also, wherever necessary, DERAC authors distinguish between narrower and wider reform positions.

Documenting judgments and deciding whether they "reach a conclusion." The DERAC authors are responsible for documenting the basis for characterizing an author's judgment. Most of the papers are loaded with quotations, while others hive off the quotations into appendices (Klein 2008; Diesel 2010). Meanwhile, many of the papers give a two-dimensional "scorecard" that tabulates types of judgment and gives the names of the authors falling within each cell (Moore and Balaker 2006; Gunter 2007; Klein 2008; Diesel 2010). The DERAC author decides whether on-record economists "reach a conclusion" on the basis of whether there is a clear preponderance of some kind.

Defining "published." For our purposes, the most essential feature in making a judgment "published" is that it is "on the record." The speaker attaches his name to the judgment. As noted, the papers vary in how widely they cast their net in canvassing for published judgments. Technological developments are making the lines of "published" somewhat blurry. A few DERAC papers include judgments found in blog posts. Some might doubt the seriousness of such discourse, but, on the other hand, such discourse is especially accountable to challenge, for example, in the comments field or at other blogs. Lines are also blurred when researchers target specific economists to respond to a questionnaire on the record.[3] Also, technology aids creation of economist petitions. Does signing a petition count as a published judgment? There has not been, to my knowledge, a petition fitting any of the 11 DERAC topics. On the other hand, the Chicago Booth Initiative on Global Markets puts its 37 economist panelists on the record. The panel has weighed in on rent control, drug policy, road pricing, and medical licensing, in each case coming to a very preponderant agreement that aligns with what the DERAC author finds on the topic.

Some Evidence of a Forsaken-Liberty Syndrome

In Table 1, there are columns summarizing whether we find on-record economists to be more pro-liberalization than at-large economists. We do find some cases of such discrepancy, which might be taken as evidence for a forsaken-liberty syndrome.

But, first, we look at three cases on which the on-record support for liberalization is high but about the same as for at-large economists. On the governmental subsidization of sports franchises, stadiums, and mega-events, Coates and Humphreys (2008) find a strong consensus among on-record economists. Meanwhile, a sample of at-large economists were asked by Whaples (2006) about whether "*Local and state governments in the U.S. should eliminate subsidies to professional sports franchises.*" Eighty-five percent either agreed (strongly or simply), and only 5 percent disagreed. It is fair to say that on-record and at-large economists are about the same on this issue. In my humble judgment, sports subsidies are an exemplary case of corporate welfare and public foolishness. On this matter, the *Journal of Economic Perspectives* has taken care to educate economists at large, publishing a fine analysis by Siegfried and Zimbalist (2000).

On rent control, Jenkins (2009) provides a thorough review of the economics literature on rent control in the United States. She writes in the abstract: "My findings cover research on many dimensions of the issue, including housing availability, maintenance and housing quality, rental rates, political and administrative costs, and redistribution. It is fair to say that the literature points to a conclusion against rent control, yet as of 2001, about 140 jurisdictions in the United States persist in some form of the intervention." These findings seem aligned to the views of at-large economists. Although no survey since 2000 has asked economists about the matter, the IGM Panel—which is a survey of 37 economists, but in which the judgment of each is *on the record*—judged very uniformly against the idea that rent control has "had a positive impact" on the amount and quality of affordable housing.

On road pricing, Lindsey (2006) provides a rich intellectual history of the idea and related policy issues. He writes in the abstract: "Practically all economists who write on the matter agree that where there is significant congestion on highways, the price should not be zero." He adds: "Beyond that primary insight, however, there is much disagreement. Economists disagree over how to set tolls, how to cover common costs, what to do with any excess revenues, whether and how 'losers' from tolling previously free roads should be compensated, and whether to privatize highways." As for at-large economists on the basic questions of road pricing, again we do not have evidence on at-large economists, but we find that the IGM Panel also strongly supports it. On the assumption that the at-large responses would be similar to the IGM Panel—though I suspect that on balance the IGM panel is a bit more liberal than economists at large—I have chalked this one up as "about the same." Thus, we figure that on three of the DERAC topics—namely, sports, rent control, and road pricing—we find strong agreement between on-record and at-large economists in favor of liberalization.

Other issues suggest evidence of a forsaken-liberty syndrome, in that the on-record economists show a stronger pattern in favor of liberalization than do the at-large economists. The strongest case is on the restrictions on drugs and devices administered by the FDA. With a few exceptions, notably Paul Krugman, I found judgment to be very preponderantly in favor of liberalization on the core issues of premarket approval, FDA control of manufacturer speech, and prescription requirements (Klein 2008). As noted previously, at-large economists appear to be considerably more favorable to FDA regulation. Further, in the survey of economics professors by Davis et al. (2011), among the 299 respondents only 42 percent opposed (strongly or not strongly) "*Tighter restrictions for the permitting of new pharmaceuticals and medical devices*."[4] Thus, there seems to be a large discrepancy between on-record and at-large economists. On this extremely important matter the *Journal of Economic Perspectives* and other AEA journals have failed to educate the at-large economists.

On medical licensing, Svorny (2004) summarizes as follows: "Economists who have examined the market for physician services in the United States generally view state licensing as a means by which to enforce cartel-like restrictions on entry that benefit physicians at the expense of consumers. Medical licensing is seen as a constraint on the efficient combination of inputs, a drag on innovations in health care and medical education, and a significant barrier to effective, cost efficient health care" (abstract). She shows that even such economists as Kenneth Arrow and Hayne Leland have made statements indicating that voluntary state certification is preferable to mandatory licensing. Meanwhile, the skepticism toward licensing is perhaps not as solid among at-large economists. When Whaples (2009: 341) asked whether "*Barriers to entering the medical profession in the U.S. should be reduced*," 64 percent of at-large economists agreed (strongly or simply), while 11 percent were neutral and 25 percent disagreed (strongly or simply). In the survey by Davis et al. (2011), only 46 percent opposed (strongly or not strongly) "*Tighter requirements on occupational licensing*."[5] I regard the discrepancy to be large, as Svorny found very few on-record economists pointing to a conclusion against reducing such barriers. The general topic of occupational licensing is scandalously understudied.[6] The *Journal of Economic Perspectives* published a nice piece on the topic by Morris M. Kleiner (2000), but the topic deserves much more attention. Incidentally, Kleiner has since published what is now probably the best current book on the topic (Kleiner 2006).

On postal reform, Geddes (2004) focuses on 10 economists who, in his judgment, have been those most prominent in economic research on the topic. He writes: "The ten vital economists surveyed here express surprisingly similar opinions on the proper direction for postal reform. The vast majority advocate some combination of privatization and elimination or relaxation of the delivery monopoly" (abstract). Geddes also treats the judgments of two economists who have not done research on the topic, Paul Samuelson and Joseph Stiglitz, both of whom are vaguely favorable to the post office and certainly do not indicate support for weakening the monopoly privileges. As for at-large economists, when Whaples (2006) asked whether "*The legal monopoly held by U.S. Postal Service (USPS) on the delivery of first class mail should be ended*," only 43 percent agreed (strongly or simply), while 25 percent were neutral and 32 percent disagreed (strongly or simply).

Next we turn to two cases in which on-record economists are "mildly more supportive of liberalization," as stated in Table 1. The comparisons are only rough. In these two cases, we see economists leaning toward liberalization, but I will suggest that in each case the on-record economists seem to lean that way somewhat more than the at-large economists.

The federal government bans payments to organ donors. Diesel (2010) writes: "I classify 72 economists and find that most of those economists who publish a judgment favor liberalization to one extent or another" (abstract). As for at-large economists, when Whaples (2009) asked whether "*The U.S. should allow payments to organ donors and their families*," 70 percent agreed (strongly or simply), while 14 percent were neutral and 16 percent disagreed (strongly or simply). In the survey by Davis et al. (2011), only 45 percent opposed (strongly or not strongly) "*Tighter restrictions on the buying and selling of human organs*." The on-record economists seem to be somewhat more pro-liberalization.

On the issue of illicit drugs, Thornton (2004) provides an extensive review of published judgments and finds a clear preponderance in favor of decriminalization and, to a lesser extent, legalization. Any comparison with at-large economists will be quite inexact, since the issues vary by the drugs treated and the reforms proposed. When "hard" drugs are specified, a slight *majority* of at-large economists (strongly or mildly) support controls on such drugs (Klein and Stern 2006: 335). In the survey by Davis et al. (2011), 49 percent opposed (strongly or not strongly) "*Tighter restrictions on 'hard' drugs such as cocaine and heroin*." But when Whaples (2006) asked whether "*The U.S. should legalize marijuana*," a slight majority agree (strongly or simply), and the IGM Panel judges even more favorably toward a "Netherlands" approach on "soft drugs." On the whole, Thornton's findings indicate a pattern among on-record economists that is somewhat more consistently supportive of liberalization.

Finally, there are three papers that do not provide evidence of a forsaken-liberty syndrome. On taxi deregulation, Moore and Balaker (2006) summarize as follows: "Here we provide a tour of the main points of contention in the scholarly research on the desirability of taxi deregulation. We find that most economic studies of taxi deregulation find it to be on net beneficial. . . . The support for taxi deregulation is preponderant, but not overwhelmingly so. We suggest that the literature favorable to deregulation is richer and broader than the unfavorable literature, which disproportionately is model-building. There is wide consensus that taxi deregulation has been less impressive than advocates had hoped" (abstract). Meanwhile, none of the surveys of economists at large have asked about taxi deregulation.

On government operation or subsidization of rail transit, Balaker and Kim (2006) deal with complexities of the issue and summarize as follows: "Of those economists who offer a big-picture view, there appears to be wide, though not unanimous, agreement that rail's costs exceed its benefits. And it seems that almost all economists who write about rail agree that various demographic features, such as suburbanization, the declining influence of central business districts, and increasing wealth will make it increasingly difficult to design successful rail systems" (abstract). Again, none of the surveys of economists at large have asked about the issue. I would guess that at-large economists would be less opposed to government subsidies than the on-record economists, but I have no evidence for the suspicion.

On household and municipal recycling, Matthew Gunter (2007) used Econlit, Google, and the library catalog to locate on-record judgments, and he organizes and tabulates the results showing a range of views and no consensus, and certainly not in favor of liberalization. The amorphous results do not conflict with what we know about how at-large economists judge the matter. When Whaples (2009) asked whether "*Laws mandating municipal curbside recycling should be eliminated*," only 25 percent agreed (strongly or simply), while 58 percent disagreed (strongly or simply).

In sum, several of the 11 DERAC papers have found no apparent difference between on-record and at-large economists, but up to five find on-record judgment to be at least somewhat more consistently pro-liberalization. I proceed to discuss whether this test is meaningful, and what it might mean.

Ruminations, Confessions, and Concluding Remarks

It would be natural for a skeptic to object as follows: "We know that the researchers involved in DERAC are staunch believers in the free market. Even if we grant the findings of the studies provided, what about the studies *not provided*? What about cases in which it would be found that on-record economists are *less* pro-liberalization than at-large economists? We cannot count on you to turn those up for us."

The *ad hominem* is sound and proper, and the logic is flawless. There may well be cases in which on-record economists show a consensus in favor of some intervention, while the at-large economists are less favorable to the intervention.

My own suspicion is that there are no such cases. It would be very interesting to query economists of various ideological stripes about whether they might postulate any such cases, or whether they agree that such cases are probably an empty set. Would any economist dispute my suspicion?

My view of the matter, in the broadest terms, is that human culture generally, and in particular Anglo-American culture since the great transformation epitomized by the passings from President Cleveland to Presidents Roosevelt, Wilson, and Roosevelt, and from Prime Minister Gladstone to Prime Ministers Asquith and George, has numerous strong biases that tend toward the under-appreciation of liberalism. Plain talk of liberty and coercion are indeed matters of great taboo. But that does not mean that such ideas are not playing a fundamental role in people's thinking and judgments.[7] The taboos and biases propel the establishment of very bad policies, which are culturally protected by notions that will not, upon responsible scrutiny, pass muster on customary standards of social betterment—for example, in my view, drug prohibition, occupational licensing, the prohibition of cash payments to organ donors, and the restrictions administered by the FDA make us less healthy, less wealthy, and less secure. I see the taboos and biases as so deep and pervasive that I do not expect even on-record economists to arrive at and state plainly good judgment on the root matters of the issue. Still, liberal enlightenment works to check the train of folly and I find some topics on which most on-record economists still get right the direction for reform. Thus, in my view, it is not likely that scholars who bear the responsibility of going on the record would come to conclusions that are less liberal than those of the general public or its subgroup, economists at large.

If, then, we accept the idea that there is among economists a forsaken-liberty syndrome, illustrated by several of the DERAC papers, and we ask why it exists, the answer, I say, must be but a part of a much larger discussion about why the vast majority of people vastly under-appreciate the presumption of liberty. Economists at large are but part of a much larger problem, and the diagnosis would reach far beyond their precincts. Many economists operate within and are the products of cultural ecologies enveloped by the apparatuses of government intervention, and their work should be interpreted accordingly.[8]

Consider the American Economic Association. It is an establishment-oriented, professional organization, and as such it is normal that it would be oriented toward the status quo. We should not expect that it would elevate those who think that many government agencies and interventions are wrongheaded at root and should be abolished. Moreover, the AEA is run by elite academics. My impression is that in the matter of ideological sensibilities the economics profession has been trending toward the academic norm, and that it will continue to do so.[9] Also, we should bear in mind that many or even most of the founders of the AEA were progressives, nationalists, or social democrats (on Richard T. Ely, see Thies and Daza 2011).

Enlightenment has a force of its own, and sometimes it will match the forces that work against it. Just as Bentham eventually carried the day on ceilings on interest rates, latter-day and, alas, now dissident liberal economists have no doubt altered the balance between the presumption of the status quo and the presumption of liberty, for example, on international trade, agricultural subsidies, drug prohibition, school vouchers, and conscription.[10] Perhaps economic enlightenment will spread on some issues, such as sports subsidies, organ policy, occupational licensing, and the FDA.

But it would be foolhardy to suppose that academia provides a setting in which enlightenment has the upper hand. Surely the minority who uphold a presumption of liberty will remain vital and make their voices heard, but their discourse might still be regarded as a sort of dissidence. Even in the heyday of the liberal era, William Gladstone in 1878 sized up academia as follows: "I trace in the education of Oxford of my own time one great defect. Perhaps it was my own fault; but I must admit that I did not learn, when at Oxford, that which I have learned since, viz., to set a due value on the imperishable and inestimable principles of human liberty. The temper which, I think, too much prevailed in academic circles, was to regard liberty with jealousy and fear . . ." (Gladstone quoted in Cook 2008: 86).

Notes

1. Specifically, 48.9 percent chose "Support strongly," 21.2 percent chose "Support mildly," 15.5 percent "Have mixed feelings," 8.3 percent chose "Oppose mildly," and 5.7 percent chose "Oppose strongly." Raw numbers are provided in Klein and Stern (2006: 334).

2. There is another paper in the DERAC section of *Econ Journal Watch*, namely Briones and Rockoff (2005), that is not treated in the present article. It is about whether economists reach a conclusion about the success of free-banking episodes in history, not about the policy issue itself. Also, one of the 11 papers treated here, namely Klein (2008), is located in a section of the journal other than DERAC, simply because it would fit in two sections and had to be located in one or the other.

3. Subsequent to my 2008 article on the FDA, Jason Briggeman, Kevin Rollins, and I designed an online survey about "pre-market approval," the banning of new drugs and devices until individually permitted by the FDA. We publicly called 305 health scholars, mostly economists, to respond on the record to the questionnaire (Klein and Briggeman 2010), and we pestered each of them with repeated emails. Of the 305 economists contacted, 44 responded. Of those, 23 supported pre-market approval (Briggeman, Klein, and Rollins 2010). Should the responses from the economists among them be counted as published judgments in favor of pre-market approval? In my view they should be heavily discounted. At any rate, the investigation might provide an example of how a line of cultural analysis can be self-subverting.

4. In this paper I report the results on four questions of the Davis et al. (2011) survey, but the reported results are not actually provided by that paper. The survey data will be provided online soon and can be obtained from me.

5. Meanwhile, the IGM Panel was very preponderantly favorable to loosening range-of-service restrictions on licensed practitioners in health care. This makes for a rough comparison with the at-large surveys, indicating that the IGM Panel is a bit more liberal than economists at large.

6. On the scant treatment of occupational licensing in labor economics textbooks, see Stephenson and Wendt (2009).

7. Hedengren, Klein, and Milton (2010) analyze the 10,792 signatures of 6,030 different individuals on 35 economist petitions, and they turn up the remarkable finding that, above a moderate threshold for being active in

signing petitions, virtually every individual signs at least quite preponderantly either in line with the liberty principle or against it. This result indicates that the liberty principle is very central in the judgment of economists, or at least those who sign petitions.

8. *Econ Journal Watch* articles that treat of this matter include White (2005), Klein with DiCola (2004), and Pasour (2004).

9. McEachern (2006) provides data on campaign contributions during the 2004 election cycle. The data strongly indicate that the elites of the AEA supported the Democratic Party vastly more than the Republican Party and that the lopsidedness increases the higher up we go in the AEA structure. As for the ideological sensibilities of the AEA membership at large, Klein et al. (2012: 153) find that it is like the general population of U.S. economics professors.

10. We think, of course, of Milton Friedman. On the role of economists, especially Friedman, in the end of military conscription, see Henderson (2005).

References

Balaker, T., and C. J. Kim. (2006). "Do Economists Reach a Conclusion on Rail Transit?" *Econ Journal Watch* 3(3): 551–602. http://econjwatch.org/articles/do-economists-reach-a-conclusion-on-rail-transit.

Bastiat, F. (1964). *Selected Essays in Political Economy*. Ed. G. B. de Huszar, trans. S. Cain. Princeton: D. Van Nostrand.

Bentham, J. (2008). Gulphs in Mankind's Career of Prosperity: A Critique of Adam Smith on Interest Rate Restrictions. [An extract of *Defence of Usury*]. *Econ Journal Watch* 5(1): 66–77. http://econjwatch.org/articles/gulphs-in-mankind-s-career-of-prosperity-a-critique-of-adam-smith-on-interest-rate-restrictions.

Briggeman, J., D. B. Klein, and K. D. Rollins. (2010). "44 Economists Answer Questionnaire on the Pre-Market Approval of Drugs and Devices." *Econ Journal Watch* 7(2): 162–173. http://econjwatch.org/articles/44-economists-answer-questionnaire-on-the-pre-market-approval-of-drugs-and-devices.

Briones, I., and H. Rockoff. (2005). "Do Economists Reach a Conclusion on Free-Banking Episodes?" *Econ Journal Watch* 2(2): 279–324. http://econjwatch.org/articles/do-economists-reach-a-conclusion-on-free-banking-episodes.

Coates, Dennis, and Brad R. Humphreys. (2008). "Do Economists Reach a Conclusion on Subsidies for Sports Franchises, Stadiums, and Mega-Events?" *Econ Journal Watch* 5(3): 294–315. http://econjwatch.org/articles/do-economists-reach-a-conclusion-on-subsidies-for-sports-franchises-stadiums-and-mega-events.

Cook, R. B. (2008). *The Grand Old Man, or, the Life and Public Services of the Right Honorable William Ewart Gladstone, Four Times Prime Minister of England.* Publishers' Union. First published 1898.

Davis, W. L., B. Figgins, D. Hedengren, and D. B. Klein. (2011). "Economics Professors' Favorite Economic Thinkers, Journals, and Blogs (Along with Party and Policy Views)." *Econ Journal Watch* 8(2): 126–146. http://econjwatch.org/articles/economics-professors-favorite-economic-thinkers-journals-and-blogs-along-with-party-and-policy-views.

Diesel, J. (2010). "Do Economists Reach a Conclusion on Organ Liberalization?" *Econ Journal Watch* 7(3): 32–336. http://econjwatch.org/articles/do-economists-reach-a-conclusion-on-organ-liberalization.

Fuller, D., and D. Geide-Stevenson. (2003). "Consensus Among Economists: Revisited." *Journal of Economic Education* 34 (4): 369–387.

Geddes, R. (2004). "Do Vital Economists Reach a Conclusion on Postal Reform?" *Econ Journal Watch* 1(1): 61–81. http://econjwatch.org/articles/postal-reform.

Gunter, M. (2007). "Do Economists Reach a Conclusion on Household and Municipal Recycling?" *Econ Journal Watch* 4(1): 83–111. http://econjwatch.org/articles/do-economists-reach-a-conclusion-on-household-and-municipal-recycling.

Hedengren, D., D. B. Klein, and C. Milton. (2010). "Economist Petitions: Ideology Revealed." *Econ Journal Watch* 7(3): 288–319. http://econjwatch.org/articles/economist-petitions-who-is-signing-what.

Henderson, D. R. (2005). "The Role of Economists in Ending the Draft." *Econ Journal Watch* 2(2): 362–376. http://econjwatch.org/articles/the-role-of-economists-in-ending-the-draft

IGM Panel. Initiative on Global Markets at the University of Chicago Booth School of Business. http://www.igmchicago.org/igm-economic-experts-panel.

Jenkins, B. (2009). "Rent Control: Do Economists Agree?" *Econ Journal Watch* 6(1): 73–112. http://econjwatch.org/articles/rent-control-do-economists-agree.

Klein, D. B. (2008). "Colleagues, Where Is the Market Failure? Economists on the FDA." *Econ Journal Watch* 5(3): 316–348. http://econjwatch.org/articles/colleagues-where-is-the-market-failure-economists-on-the-fda.

Klein, D. B., and J. Briggeman. (2010). "305 Economists Called to Answer Questionnaire on the Pre-Market Approval of Drugs and Devices." *Econ Journal Watch* 7(1): 99–106. http://econjwatch.org/articles/305-economists-called-to-answer-questionnaire-on-the-pre-market-approval-of-drugs-and-devices.

Klein, D. B., W. L. Davis, B. G. Figgins, and D. Hedengren. (2012). "Characteristics of the Members of Twelve Economic Associations: Voting, Policy Views, and Favorite Economists." *Econ Journal Watch* 9(2): 149–162.

http://econjwatch.org/articles/characteristics-of-the-members-of-twelve-economics-associations-voting-policy-views-and-favorite-economists.

Klein, D. B., with T. DiCola. (2004). "Institutional Ties of *Journal of Development Economics* Authors and Editors." *Econ Journal Watch* 1(2): 319–330. http://econjwatch.org/articles/institutional-ties-of-journal-of-development-economics-authors-and-editors.

Klein, D. B., and C. Stern. (2005). "Professors and Their Politics: The Policy Views of Social Scientists." *Critical Review* 17 (3/4): 257–303. http://www.criticalreview.com/2004/pdfs/klein_stern.pdf.

——. (2006). "Economists' Policy Views and Voting." *Public Choice* 126: 331–342.

——. (2007). "Is There a Free-Market Economist in the House? The Policy Views of American Economic Association Members." *American Journal of Economics and Sociology* 66(2): 309–334. http://www.gmu.edu/departments/economics/klein/PdfPapers/Klein-SternAJES%202007.pdf.

Kleiner, M. M. (2000). "Occupational Licensing." *Journal of Economic Perspective* 14(4): 189–202.

——. (2006). *Licensing Occupations: Ensuring Quality or Restricting Competition?* Kalamazoo, MI: W.E. Upjohn Institute for Employment Research.

Kuran, T. (1995). *Private Truths, Public Lies: The Social Consequences of Preference Falsification.* Cambridge, MA: Harvard University Press.

Lindsey, R. (2006). "Do Economists Reach a Conclusion on Road Pricing? The Intellectual History of an Idea." *Econ Journal Watch* 3(2): 292–379. http://econjwatch.org/articles/do-economists-reach-a-conclusion-on-road-pricing-the-intellectual-history-of-an-idea.

May, A. M., and R. Whaples. (Forthcoming). "Are Disagreements Between Male and Female Economists Marginal at Best?: A Survey of AEA Members and Their Views on Economics and Economic Policy." *Contemporary Economic Policy.*

McEachern, W. A. (2006). "AEA Ideology: Campaign Contributions of American Economic Association Members, Committee Members, Officers, Editors, Referees, Authors, and Acknowledgees." *Econ Journal Watch* 3(1): 148–179. http://econjwatch.org/articles/aea-ideology-campaign-contributions-of-american-economic-association-members-committee-members-officers-editors-referees-authors-and-acknowledgees.

Mises, L. von (1966). *Human Action.* Chicago: Henry Regnery.

Moore, A., and T. Balaker. (2006). "Do Economists Reach a Conclusion on Taxi Deregulation?" *Econ Journal Watch* 3(1): 109–132. http://econjwatch.org/articles/do-economists-reach-a-conclusion-on-taxi-deregulation.

Pasour, E. C., Jr. (2004). "Agricultural Economists and the State." *Econ Journal Watch* 1(1): 106–133. http://econjwatch.org/articles/agricultural-economists-and-the-state.

Siegfried, J., and A. Zimbalist. (2000). "The Economics of Sports Facilities and Their Communities." *Journal of Economic Perspectives* 14(3): 95–114.

Stephenson, E. F., and E. E. Wendt. (2009). "Occupational Licensing: Scant Treatment in Labor Texts." *Econ Journal Watch* 6(2): 181–194. http://econjwatch.org/articles/occupational-licensing-scant-treatment-in-labor-texts.

Svorny, S. (2004). "Licensing Doctors: Do Economists Agree?" *Econ Journal Watch* 1(2): 279–305. http://econjwatch.org/articles/licensing-doctors-do-economists-agree.

Thies, C. F., and R. Daza. (2011). "Richard T. Ely: The Confederate Flag of the AEA?" *Econ Journal Watch* 8(2): 147–156. http://econjwatch.org/articles/richard-t-ely-the-confederate-flag-of-the-aea.

Thornton, Mark. (2004). "Prohibition vs. Legalization: Do Economists Reach a Conclusion on Drug Policy?" *Econ Journal Watch* 1(1): 82–105. http://econjwatch.org/articles/drug-policy.

Viner, J. (1927). "Adam Smith and Laissez-Faire." *Journal of Political Economy* 35(2): 198–232.

Whaples, R. (2006). "Do Economists Agree on Anything? Yes!" *Economists' Voice* 3(9): art 1. http://www.bepress.com/cgi/viewcontent.cgi?filename=0&article=1156&context=ev&type=additional.

——. (2009). "The Policy Views of American Economic Association Members: The Results of a New Survey." *Econ Journal Watch* 6(3): 337–348. http://econjwatch.org/articles/the-policy-views-of-american-economic-association-members-the-results-of-a-new-survey.

White, L. H. (2005). "The Federal Reserve System's Influence on Research in Monetary Economics." *Econ Journal Watch* 2(2): 325–354. http://econjwatch.org/articles/the-federal-reserve-system-s-influence-on-research-in-monetary-economics.

Wootton, B. (1938). *Lament for Economics.* London: George Allen & Unwin.

Index

for

DIFFERENT BUT EQUAL: DOCUMENTING THE CONTRIBUTION OF DISSIDENT SCHOLARS